Creative Rituals
AN ART WITCH GUIDEBOOK

Creative Rituals
AN ART WITCH GUIDEBOOK

by Laura Gyre

ARABI MANOR

A REBEL SATORI IMPRINT

New Orleans

Published in the United States of America and United Kingdom by

Rebel Satori Press

www.rebelsatoripress.com

Copyright © 2023 Laura Gyre All rights reserved. Except for brief passages quoted in newspaper, magazine, radio, television, or online reviews, no part of this book may be reproduced in any form or any means, electronic or mechanical, including photocopying, recording, or information or retrieval system, without the permission in writing from the publisher. Please do not participate in or encourage piracy of copyrighted materials in violation of the author's rights. Purchase only authorized editions.

Paperback ISBN: 978-1-60864-168-0

To all my magical teachers and to James,
who has always believed in this project.

Margaret Wallace was a bad woman
and she burned, in Scotland, 1622.

Blood spilled over witches in those days
more easily than ink, but
the charges were the usual:
consulting a known witch, healing,
maleficium and neighborhood dispute.
Heavy on the neighborhood dispute, and maleficium?

An evil, misdeed, wickedness, offense, crime, hurt,
harm, wrong, enchantment or sorcery. By definition,
almost, her crime was that bad,
and she may have been burning too much
before or after her execution.
Before or after her execution
her body was consigned to the flames—
but the souls of witches are inflammable,
and so, Margaret Wallace, intercede for us.

Save us from this kind of definition.
Save us from this kind of definition.

Give us a witchcraft that burns from the inside.

Beginnings

This is a map. It's a magical map. It's also one of the oldest (as old as recorded history) and most widely-used human symbols, found everywhere from Europe to the Americas, Africa and Asia. The specific meaning varies from place to place, and in some cases is entirely lost to time. However, there does seem to be a common thread that runs through many interpretations:

We are each, wherever we may be, at the center of our own world—and we are surrounded by powerful forces which are, and must remain, in balance.

I learned about this symbol while studying Witchcraft, which is hard to define but tends to be a family of magical systems influenced by European folk tradition and pagan or animist roots. These systems lean heavily on the power of story and imagery, which have helped to preserve a variety of amazing old teachings that are still totally relevant today.

There is no (one) holy book of Witchcraft, no government or council deciding who can or can't be a witch. This lack of discrimination can lead to some serious weirdness around the edges. We are, and have always been, a fairly diverse and not entirely reputable bunch, and as much as we might like to write off fraudulent palm readers or cheesy lifestyle brands, there has never been any obvious place to draw a line. Attempts to do so tend to come off as sanctimonious—if not entirely contrary to the spirit of the endeavor—anyway, and this quality has probably added to our overall mystique. Are we all just a bunch of deluded idiots and opportunistic frauds, or aren't we? As much as bystanders might like to know, the only way to find out, really, is to stop hanging around at the edges and head straight for the center of the map—which may be just as well in the end.

In the world of European magic this circular symbol is best known as a map of the elemental realms, coming to us from ancient Greece by way of the medieval alchemists. Specifically, the first record of our four magical elements (earth, water, air and fire) comes from the Greek philosopher Empedocles. Empedocles believed that all matter in the universe was made up of these four elements. and in a way he was correct (though today we might say that all matter consists of solid, liquid, gas and plasma). However, like most magical models the elemental map can and should be understood on a variety of different levels.

For our purposes, it's most important to consider the elemental qualities that each of us possesses: a rational mind (clear and bright, like air), a solid, earthy body, a deep, subconscious well of creativity and…well, it gets a bit complicated with fire, but we'll get into that later. In the meantime, the important thing is the idea of bringing those elements into communication and balance.

From a spiritual perspective, there is magic and interconnection in all things, all the time—but I certainly find that when I pay attention to the lessons of the elemental wheel, doing my best to develop all four qualities and keep them somewhat in balance, I'm in a better place (the center of the universe) to tune in to that magic and allow it to unfold naturally. This emergent quality is what an alchemist might call the *quintessence*, or the fifth element of spirit, and it's what this book is about.

Or at least, that's how I see it. I do want to mention before we get too much further, that what I'm setting down here is entirely my own perspective. Of course, it's very deeply informed by the lessons of many teachers and people I've met along the way, from inside and outside the Witchcraft tradition.

For example, when I was in my early twenties and trying to figure out where I fit in spiritually, I attended a month-long Buddhist retreat that changed my life. Two things really stuck with me: the value of a hundred or so hours of meditation, and the way the teacher was always telling us to check up on everything. "Don't take my word for it," he would say, while discussing the varieties of demons and heavenly realms, "Check up! Just try it and see how it works in your life." Regardless of my personal feelings about demons, it actually did work really well and he had a point.

I'm not at all qualified to teach Buddhism, though I do have a few favorite exercises that have stuck with me as part of my personal practice. You know what works even better in my life, though?

Witchcraft.

So, I'd like to offer all that follows in a similar spirit. Read the notes, do the exercises, but most of all, check up! See how you feel, what you think, and especially what happens next. With that in mind, I've decided to dive right into the magical stuff: using the elemental map to cast spells.

The basics are surprisingly simple but there are endless libraries of magical theory out there, and I spend a lot of my spare time sorting through them and experimenting. I've made a lot of notes on a lot of related subjects—particularly about the sort of "aha" moments when a certain idea finally clicked into place for me, but also about some favorite recipes, rituals and specialized tools. I've tried to plug all that in where it might be relevant, mystic grimoire hodge-podge style.

Skeptic's Note:

This book is absolutely about real magic. Possible side-effects may include surprising coincidence, lucky breaks, psychic communication, prophetic dreams, spontaneous healing and dazzling experiences of cosmic oneness. It's also about psychology, neurobiology, productivity, healthy habits and creative excellence. If it's very important to you, you're welcome to read along and imagine that all this magic stuff is metaphorical—as long as you're totally sure that that will be more fun.

ON MAGIC AND HOT AIR BALLOONS

What do we mean when we talk about magic? We'll get deeper into theory in the next section, but I like to think about it like a hot air balloon. Of course, the balloon floats because it's filled with hot air. But did you ever wonder about how it's steered? On some level it actually isn't. Instead, the air around it is full of invisible currents, going in all sorts of directions all the time. So, as a balloon pilot you just watch the signs (smoke trails, flags, and so on) to see which direction the wind is moving above and below you. All you can do is turn the fire up or down to raise or lower the balloon, into the current that's already going your way.

When I heard about this, it sounded exactly like how magic works to me. I'm not going to tell you that magical practice can get you absolutely anything in the world (though, I hope you'll prove me wrong, and write and tell me about how it worked out). But I will tell you that there are a million possible futures that you can't even imagine swirling around you right now, and if you start to pay attention in the right way you'll become more and more aware of which small choices can make a big, surprising difference in where you might eventually end up. Plus, of course, you'll be in a hot air balloon, so you should have a lot of fun along the way.

ON WITCHCRAFT AND WICCA

In case these terms are new to you, and especially because there's some cultural baggage attached to Witches and Witchcraft, I can (sort of) clarify what I do and don't mean when I talk about Witchcraft. Basically, what I mean is a spiritual path that's based on magical practice. Witches study and (usually) practice magic, as a way to understand the world, actively participate in the mystical universe, improve our life circumstances and generally make things more interesting.

While there are magical traditions worldwide, those who choose to call themselves Witches are usually drawing somewhat on a variety of related mystical currents that were passed down in Europe over the centuries—though, at this point, these traditions have grown and transformed in a variety of different ways. Very few practices have continued in an unbroken lineage from antiquity, and many have been influenced by teachings from other parts of the world. At this point, a lot of modern innovations like the study of biology, psychology and other contemporary arts and sciences have made their way into the stream, too. It's also worth noting the connection to alchemy again, as this paragraph in particular could describe either tradition. The fact is, there's no clear line between the two, though Witchcraft tends to be more folky and intuitive, and alchemy more philosophically rigorous and focused on things like elemental maps and recipes. So, I do owe a great deal to the alchemical tradition personally, and if you want to get technical my work tends to fall somewhere in the area between the two.

If you've heard much about Witchcraft before, you might have heard that it's the same as the religion Wicca, which is confusing and only sort of true. Basically, Wicca started out as a religious practice in the mid 1900s, based on what some English people at that time believed traditional Witchcraft had been like—meaning, Wicca is *one* valid form of Witchcraft practice, though many Wiccans prefer not to use that word because of the negative connotations. Over the past century, Wicca itself has grown and diversified a great deal, too, but still tends to focus a lot on religious worship—usually of a goddess, god and goddess, or a variety of gods. I'm very grateful to the Wiccan movement for bringing magical practice into popular consciousness, and particularly to those of my teachers who have identified as Wiccan Witches. There is some material in this book that has come to me more or less through that tradition, but I'm not particularly aiming (or even qualified, there's often a formal lineage involved) to teach Wicca.

Chaos magic is another twentieth-century trend that's worth a mention here, because it helped to introduce the idea that magic is a really personal practice, and a lot of the dogma and prescribed ritual that has grown up around occult traditions can be disposed with if it doesn't resonate for you, to be replaced by your own experience and intuition. I don't identify as a chaos magician because, as much as I love these ideas, a lot of the modern culture that has grown up around them tends, ironically, toward particular structures and practices, and in general I prefer the flavor of Witchcraft—but some of my favorite magical folks are into chaos magic, and I think we have a lot in common and a lot to learn from each other.

So, is Witchcraft a religion? Sort of. Some Witches identify as atheists, agnostics or members of other religions and practice magic in a non-religious way, or under the umbrella of their faith. Besides personal identity, though, this question comes down to your definition of religion. A lot of people with Christian backgrounds tend to assume that a religion is based on *orthodoxy*, or shared belief—which isn't necessarily the case worldwide. Some religions, especially older animist traditions, are less defined by shared belief than by *orthopraxy*: a shared sense of spiritual practice and behavior. Witchcraft is entirely orthopractic, with no prescribed set of beliefs. For me, it functions very much like a religion, but your mileage may vary.

ON THE ELEMENTAL MAP

One complicated thing—maybe the most complicated thing—about magical theory and practice is that, unlike something like history or math, there's no obvious starting point. This is the lesson of the ouroboros, the alchemical image of the snake swallowing its own tail. Everything is connected, and everything builds on everything else, so you pretty much have to jump in before you feel entirely ready.

If I had to pick just one bit of magical lore to share with the world, though, it would probably be this elemental model. For one thing, it can be used as a more literal map, by assigning each element to a corner or direction. This is a mainstay of Wiccan practice, and practitioners often begin rituals by walking in a circle, calling to the elemental powers in each of the four directions.

Here, we'll be focusing more on the elemental aspects of human experience. The book is organized into elemental sections, allowing you to go in order and work through all four elements, or skip around to focus more on the elements you choose.

There are a few different traditions about the ways the elements are arranged when they're laid out in a circle. The first one that I learned was along geographical lines. For practitioners working in Europe, it would be easy to imagine fiery warmth to the south, watery ocean to the west, cold, bare earth to the north and light, airy things like the morning star in the east (also, air in the east somewhat by process of elimination). This is a common, but certainly not universal arrangement of the elements. Another common one, especially among Wiccans, is to assign the elements to the five points of a star rather than the four points of a circle, with the fifth (usually top) point representing spirit. This is related to the use of the pentacle (pentagram inside a circle) as a symbol of Witchcraft. Personally, I usually prefer to stick to a four-primary-element model, leaving spirit in the center.

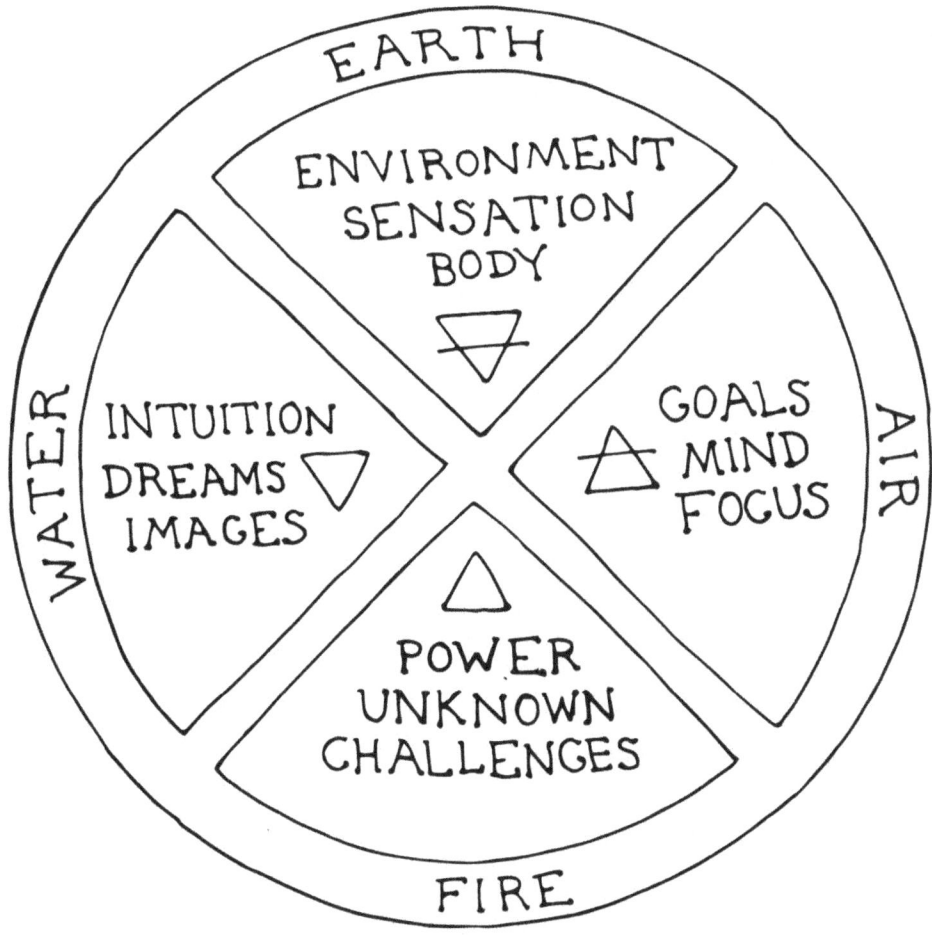

Some people feel it makes more intuitive sense to use water opposite fire, and air (probably up) opposite earth (probably down), and I tend to agree that this feels intuitive. There's a historical reason that this isn't usually the case, though. The alchemists traditionally assigned the qualities warm, cool, wet and dry to the elements. So far, so good, right? However, they assigned *two* of those qualities to each element. So, fire was both warm and dry, while earth was cold and dry, etc. Then, rather than placing fire opposite water, they placed cool opposite dry and so on, which led to the most common arrangement. Unless you're planning to get deep into alchemy or energetic herbalism, you will probably never need to know about this. Still, there's a power to doing things in the way they have been done for hundreds of years,

On the other hand, there's a power to doing them in a way that makes sense to your modern mind, and unfortunately, like many systems in witchcraft, there's no perfect way of making all that line up (so the map can never be the territory). Fortunately, a lot of us eventually come around to feeling that that's a feature rather than a defect. Most of the maps work quite well on a practical level, and it's good to be reminded to look up once in a while and orient yourself according to your own inner sense of direction.

ON MAGICAL JOURNALING

I would highly, highly recommend starting your magical journey with some kind of journal or sketchbook. This doesn't have to be anything fancy (though it can be, if you're looking for an excuse to buy a fancy journal). Blank, unlined paper is nice, so you can draw as well as write. You can definitely get creative and do it art journal style if you want.

One of my own favorite magical journals is actually a three-ring binder, which has a few advantages: you can add a custom cover image if you want (a lot of standard three-ring binders have a plastic cover you can slide a sheet of paper under), create any combination of lined and blank paper, add pages of content you print out or photocopy (there are a few templates for that kind of thing in this book) or even include plastic sleeves to hold magazine clippings or other flat stuff you might want to use eventually. You can divide the paper into as many sections as you want (and change your mind repeatedly) *and* you can get that blank book feeling any time by getting rid of any pages or sections you've changed your mind about.

Really, though, almost any kind of book will work. I prefer the feeling of writing and sketching my magical notes out by hand, but you can even do your journaling on a computer, or by audio or video recording if that works better for you.

Once you pick your method and materials, start making magical notes. When you work on the exercises in this book, write down exactly what you did, how it felt, what you learned and what you might do the same or differently in the future. Also start to check in once a day or so, just to write down any new thoughts, notes on things you've read, or experiences you've had that felt especially magical. This is a really useful record to have, so you can easily look back and see what you've learned, how your life is changing, and eventually which practices are working out the best for you.

As you make these notes, feel free to take creative liberties. One of the paradoxical things that happens when you start to practice magic is that you don't quite believe in it because you haven't seen enough evidence yet—but when your evidence starts to show up, you're not sure if it's magical enough because you have nothing to compare it to. So, for now, assume that if it *feels* magical, that's good enough. Would you say you experienced a magical moment when you saw that breathtaking sunset, or your favorite song suddenly started to play at a meaningful time? It's fine to fake it till you make it. In fact, it's pretty much required.

ON MAKING A BLANK BOOK

If you're feeling crafty and/or eager to get started right away, here's a simple kind of book you can make yourself.

Materials:

- regular office paper, maybe about 15 sheets

- thin cardboard like a cereal box, or plain card stock

- thick corrugated cardboard (a little piece is enough)

- stapler that can be opened to staple on a flat surface

- glue stick

- fancy washi tape, masking or duct tape

Fold the stack of paper in half, then open up again, with the point of the fold facing up. Place on top of the thick cardboard to protect your working surface, then open your stapler all the way and staple down in three places along the fold line. Remove the cardboard and carefully press the points of the staples closed if necessary.

Cut two 8.5" x 6.5" rectangles out of thin cardboard (if you recycle a cereal box or something similar, you can use the blank side for the outside cover). Place the paper booklet point-side-up again and glue one piece of cardboard to the front cover and one to the back.

Leaving it open on the table with the cardboard facing up, run a piece of tape along the spine to connect the two cardboard covers and cover any pointy staple bits. Fold the ends of the tape over slightly to hide them on the inside of the book.

Optionally, press the whole thing under a heavy book or other weight to flatten before using.

I. A BREATH OF FRESH AIR

Air is the element associated with the rational mind, and the mind is an important (but tricky) place to start on magical work. Our minds are immensely powerful in shaping our experiences. Regardless of your feelings about magic—whether or not you already believe that your thoughts influence the world around you—you should know that your beliefs and expectations play a huge role in how your life experience feels.

How it feels, in turn, can influence all sorts of things.

For example, the effectiveness of placebo medicine is pretty well documented. That means that if you go to a doctor for a problem and the doctor gives you a pill, your condition is suddenly more likely to improve, even if the pill is just sugar. Your belief that the medicine has the power to help you increases the chance that you will start to feel better—and feeling better and more optimistic (while certainly not a cure-all) improves your body's natural function and gives you the best possible chance of real physical healing.

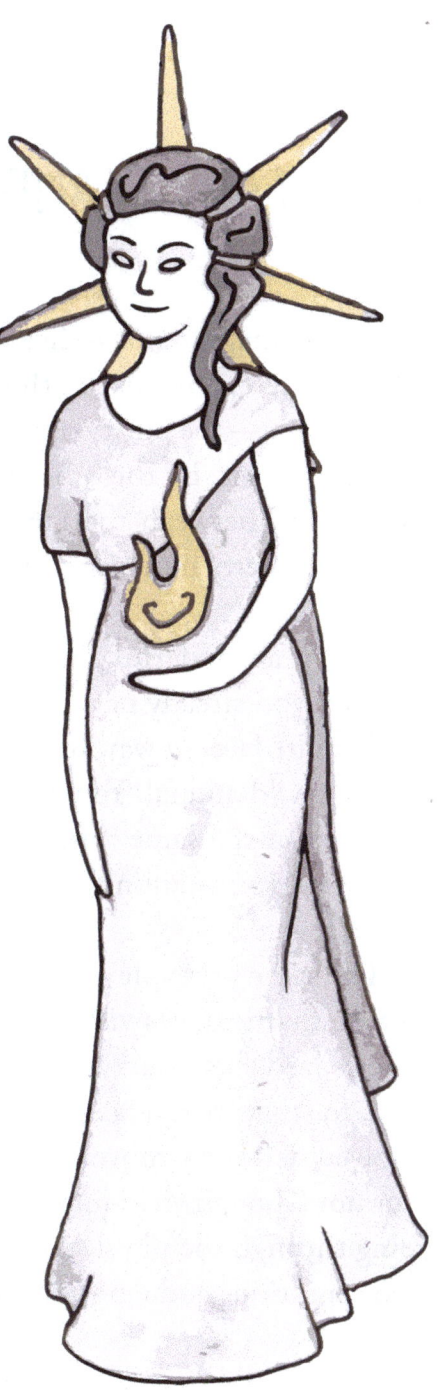

This is pretty much how a lot of magic works. It's a natural process, like healing, that tends to unfold when the conditions are right. Half the trick to increasing the magic in your life is believing that it's possible in the first place—which is why it's so important at first to treat every awesome thing in your life as evidence that you're surrounded by magic and the possibility of more magic. The other half of the trick (which can be the tough part) is staying somewhat grounded while you do that.

It's all very well to cultivate a belief in magic, but we need to do it in a way that respects our intelligence and our actual lived experiences, too. In other words, believing that you have the power to heal is good and constructive magic, but believing that you're definitely healing while you put off treatment and ignore your worsening symptoms is not. This is a fine line, and it can be difficult to walk. In fact, it's nearly impossible to walk by relying on your rational mind alone—which is why it's a good idea and a powerful magical practice to balance those elemental energies and tune in to other sources of information, like the wisdom of your body and the subconscious imagery of your dreams. For now, though, let's focus on harnessing the power of the mind.

ON CREATIVITY AND THE MAGICAL MINDSET

In general, magic tends to live in the spaces between this and that. This can be a bit of a cultural stretch, because both science and Judeo-Christian tradition tend to emphasize the opposite—the purity of each thing in its precise definition and proper place. Witchcraft and magic, on the other hand, are all about the liminal, the hedge zone (the most biodiverse!) between the forest and the meadow, the twilight hour between day and night and pretty much anything hard to pin down and define.

This is a wonderful plus for art witches. If you create art (any kind of art, even occasionally) you already have some practice with understanding things in a magically powerful, multi-faceted way. Imagine, for example, that you want to paint a picture of yourself as a wild animal. You know on some level that you don't actually have this animal body, but at the same time a part of you experiences the reality that you do—because otherwise, you wouldn't know anything about how to make the painting.

The same principle applies to other types of art, too. For example, imagine acting out a scene that involves visiting a place you've never been in real life. You haven't actually experienced that situation, but in a way you are having the experience as you act it out (and, for that matter, as you imagine acting it out right now, though getting your body involved definitely moves the experience a bit closer to reality). Whether you believe in it or not (though vivid imagination and suspension of disbelief definitely help), you are going through the physical motions of the scene and maybe feeling some of the associated sensations and emotions. For your body, in some ways, the experience is true.

Even writing can be used in a similar way. Writing is tricky because we can easily fall into totally literal and logical habits, but language can also be used paradoxically, or poetically. You can write that your love is a rose. What does that mean? Is it true or isn't it? This can get complicated, but your logical mind doesn't really have to grasp what it means in order for the phrase to work its magic.

If, as you start to work on these practices, you're troubled by a feeling that you're not sure if you believe in what you're doing, take a step backwards and look at it more like this: creative play is an incredibly powerful state that can circumvent our obsessive need to prove and disprove things. It's a sneaky way of allowing ourselves to experience the reality of things that we don't yet think we can believe are true.

Or, of course, you could just go down to the crossroads and ask for some help. Intersections, literal and figurative, are a big deal in magical lore. Like the crossed lines in the center of the elemental wheel, they evoke those spooky spaces between things, and all points where possibilities merge and diverge. If you'd like to bring more of this in-between quality into your life, visit a crossroads near your home. Try to go at a liminal time like dawn, twilight or midnight. Bring an offering if you want, or just light a candle and ask the helpful spirits and witchy ancestors to teach you what you need to know about travelling on the path of not exactly this and not exactly that. Write about what happens in your journal.

ON WITCHCRAFT AND SAFETY

When people are getting into witchcraft for the first time, their number one question tends to be *are we really going to take this seriously?* For the already-intrigued, a couple of mysterious stories are usually enough to convince them to give it a try. There's not a lot to lose, and if it doesn't work out, at least they might end up with a few interesting stories. The second common question is more troubling, though. *Is it dangerous to practice witchcraft?*

It isn't that surprising, because there are a lot of spooky ideas about magic floating around. If you're wondering if it's a bad idea for you to practice magic, the most important answer is that you certainly don't have to. Depending on your religious background you might choose not to, and occasionally people seem so concerned that I wonder why they're considering it in the first place. You probably don't need magic to achieve your goals, and the path won't necessarily be easier—just weirder and usually more fun. But, you're reading this book, so let's assume that at least a part of you wants to try it. Maybe you would like me to assure you that Witchcraft is safe and not evil.

Here's what I can say about that: Witchcraft isn't necessarily safe, but studying it might be a little safer than not studying it. If you start to develop a belief that your actions have metaphysical repercussions, well, that was probably true before you started, too, and now you might be in a better position to navigate that reality. Of course, practicing Witchcraft is no guarantee that you won't make terrible decisions and pursue goals that aren't good for you, but it's also no guarantee that you *will*. Going after those goals in a holistic, artful way might even mean that you'll learn your lessons more effectively and move along to the next thing a little more quickly. If something starts to go wrong in your life, there's a good chance that you'll notice sooner and have more tools at your disposal to address the situation.

If you're wondering whether Witchcraft is ok on a moral level, the answer might depend more on your intentions than your methods. Would it be wrong to use magic to take away someone's free will? Almost certainly. There are witches who are willing to curse under the right circumstances, but most of us would probably be willing to throw a punch under the right circumstances, too. A good rule of thumb is to think about how far you would go to accomplish your goal by other means. If you feel ok about physical action, I don't see any reason to worry that it would be wrong to achieve the same result by magic. Still, of course, you should check up—as usual, your mileage may vary.

TOWARD AN ETHICS OF WITCHCRAFT, PART 1

Many witches do believe in a concept of cause and effect somewhat similar to karma, which is worth keeping in mind when you decide on your magical intentions. This isn't the traditional Hindu version, though, or even the pop-culture version where the universe is out to punish bad guys. It's maybe more similar to poetic justice, and certainly seems to show up that way in magical stories.

I was taught that the mythical figure of Midas is a good example of how this works.

Midas was an ancient king who did a favor for the god Dionysus, who in turn offered to grant him a wish. Since he was a greedy man, Midas wished for (and was granted) the ability to turn anything he touched into gold. This worked out perfectly until he found that he couldn't touch food, flowers, or even his own daughter. In the end, he learned his lesson and begged the gods to reverse his wish.

An interesting thing about that story is that nobody set out to punish Midas—he just experienced the logical, extreme consequence of his bottomless greed. Unlike moral prescriptivism, this is the sort of natural law that witches tend to think about a lot. *Be careful what you wish for,* we say, *because you very well might get it.*

There's a Wiccan concept called *The Rule of Three*, which says that whatever you send out into the universe will actually come back to you three times more powerfully. This seems awfully specific, but it's worth considering that we're rarely aware of the full impact of our actions, and we often tend to underestimate the harm that we can cause when our intentions are good—so, assuming that any harmful or sloppy intentions you send out might have about three times the impact you expect (on yourself and everyone else) can be a decent rule of thumb.

Figuring out how all this works is usually a process of trial and error, and even Midas eventually got a second chance. From this perspective, a life of magical practice can be a continuous process of honing your core desires, which (spoiler alert) tend to be on the broadly beneficial side. What happy, healthy person wouldn't want to live in a world where others are also feeling good? This is the sense in which, while it doesn't come with a prescriptive moral code, Witchcraft can be a path of self-improvement and even of service to the world.

ON THE POWER OF YOUR WORD

On a related note, there are two important, highly intertwined personal qualities that tend to be valued by Witches: honesty and integrity. You could think of this as an ethical suggestion, but the reasons are actually quite practical. This work is all about integrity in the sense that we are working to *integrate* our mental, physical and spiritual experiences more and more deeply, attempting to get them all moving in the same direction.

That may seem like a somewhat obscure definition of integrity, but it's actually deeply related to the conventional definition. For example, doing something in private that you wouldn't want others to know about can be described as lacking integrity, and it could also be experienced as a conflict between two different parts of your being (the part that wants to do that thing, and the part that wants to be seen as someone who wouldn't). The more you integrate your diverse experiences on a magical level, the more integrity you will have on a practical level—and the more you practice the virtue of integrity, the more magically effective you will be.

Honesty operates in a similar way, and starts within yourself. If you can't admit to what you really want, for example, you'll have a hard time moving powerfully toward magical results. You also need to be realistic about what you fear (in order to work constructively with those feelings), and so on. Basically, there's a lot of inner work involved, and the foundation of all of that is a willingness to deal with what's actually going on in your life, rather than doing imaginary work on imaginary situations.

Being honest with other people is a little more advanced, and I think most of us would agree that there are extreme circumstances that call for exceptions (or at least sneaky work-arounds, like in the fairy tales). There are probably not as many of these exceptions as we like to think, though, especially when it comes to the little stuff that tends to fly under our radar: insincere compliments, convenient excuses, and things along those lines.

If you find it hard to be honest with yourself or others, I'd suggest giving that some thought and maybe some space in your journal. All this is a process, of course, but If you're hiding feelings or behavior that you're uncomfortable with, it might be time to dig into what's going on there and what you think might happen if people saw you and your real desires more clearly. Sometimes there are noble intentions involved, like a desire to make people feel good and avoid hurting feelings. Many people also value honesty, though, especially if it's delivered in a kind, constructive and non-pushy way.

Honesty and integrity are good policies in general, leading to actions and relationships that feel good because they're grounded in your actual feelings. Magically speaking, though, the bottom line is that a lot of spellwork comes down to announcing your intentions, too. The more fully you can believe in the power of your own word when you do that, the stronger a foundation you have to build on.

ON LIMITING BELIEFS

A lot of us have a huge number of limiting beliefs around magic just from living in the modern world. I'm not suggesting that we try to jump straight into believing in something totally different, because that can be really hard and isn't necessarily a good idea, anyway. But a major goal when you start to work with mental magic should be to notice how those limiting beliefs show up for you. For example, if you get ready to do a magical exercise and immediately have a bunch of thoughts like *what's the point of this? Nothing is going to happen anyway*, those are limiting beliefs you're running into.

Congratulations! It's normal and ok to have that kind of thought, and it doesn't need to hold you back. Even though I've been practicing Witchcraft for years I still have those thoughts at times, and a huge part of magical experience is learning to hold both things at once (the fact that you might have that thought and also that you can allow yourself to try the thing anyway). It's a good idea just to be aware of that process, and try to open up some space

around it. You don't have to tell yourself that you believe the magical thing is going to work, but maybe you can introduce some questions. For example: *How can I be so sure that this won't work? Anything is possible. There are plenty of things I haven't experienced, and that science hasn't figured out yet.* Usually, repeating something like this to yourself occasionally and not letting those initial thoughts paralyze you is good enough.

ON NOTICING DESIRES

You also might want to start paying more attention to your desires, as you prepare to work with them in a more deliberate way. Most of us have lots of desires over the course of each day, but we may not even notice a lot of them as they pass by. Of course, not all of the momentary desires that pass through our minds are actually good for us, and we're certainly not going to do spellwork around all of them—but we could probably stand to give them all a little more attention just so we can be more aware of what our minds are up to.

For example, if you're at work and you suddenly have a thought that you want to quit your job, it probably doesn't mean you should get up and walk out the door. It's still worth noticing that thought and taking a second to honor the desire, though. One thing thing that can happen when you start paying attention to those momentary impulses is that you may notice which ones come up again and again. If you notice that you want to quit your job several times a day, it might be time to start thinking more seriously about your options.

ON THE MAGIC OF FREE-WRITING

A great way to sort through mental stuff like limiting beliefs and confusing desires is to practice freewriting. This is different from keeping a log of your experiences, but it's another good section to put in your journal if you have the space. I've also found it to be surprisingly magical. When I first started studying Witchcraft, it wasn't until I adopted a daily practice of freewriting that I really noticed surprising things starting to shift in my life.

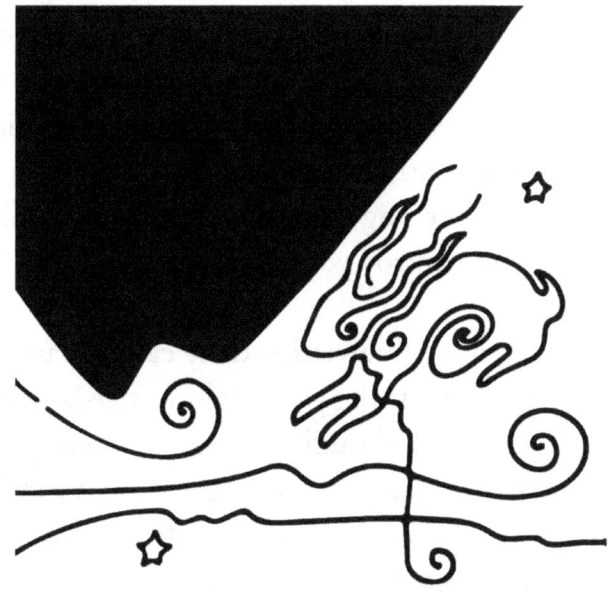

To get started, pick a quantity goal like three pages, 20 minutes or 750 words (a word count works well if you prefer to type, which is just as good, though there can be something kind of magical about writing by hand). Write about anything at all, and try not to stop until you reach your goal. If you want, you can use a journaling prompt like the ones in the next section, or you can just write down whatever is on your mind at the moment. Wherever you start, chances are that your topics will be all over the place by the time you finish (this is good). If you find yourself at a total loss for words, you can even write the same thing again and again until something new crosses your mind. It is a good idea, when you can remember it, to bring your attention back to concrete experience and writing about things you can see, taste and touch (or at least, things you can imagine seeing, tasting and touching).

Freewriting started out as an exercise for writers, but it's important to keep in mind that the point isn't to produce anything well-written. In fact, most of the time you won't even want to read this stuff again in the future (though you might want to make a couple of notes in your practice log if any interesting ideas come up). It's a great practice for witchy folks because if you take the idea of free expression really seriously you will find that things that are on your mind subconsciously (like desires, fears, and unexamined beliefs) start to float to the surface where you can see what they are and decide what you might want to do about them. Including sensory detail tends to make for stronger writing, but the reason to use it here is just to get deeply engaged in the practice, bringing your whole being into the experience more fully.

Along the way, you might notice some thoughts or feelings that really surprise or even concern you. Think of this as a learning experience, but keep in mind that just because a weird or extra-petty thought crossed your mind—like the thought that you kind of wanted to murder the person who cut you off in traffic earlier—it isn't necessarily true. Just write it down, and watch how quickly your mind will (usually) move on to the next thing, without even needing to make any effort. If you're worried about the magical impact of writing something you don't fully agree with, you can always burn, trash or otherwise destroy your writing later.

Practicing freewriting daily can be a useful experiment, especially if you haven't tried it before. One thing you might notice is that you feel most resistant at times when some uncomfortable thoughts are getting ready to surface, which is to say that the days when you feel the least like writing are often the days when it would be the most useful. Now that I'm used to that feeling, I don't always write every day, but I do tend to pull out my notebook when I start to feel confused, overwhelmed or just a bit sluggish and stuck. Journaling is a great tool for figuring out what's going on with a tricky situation and starting to plan how to move forward, magically and otherwise.

A MONTH OF PROMPTS FOR MAGICAL JOURNALING

You can start journaling wherever you like, but if you want some inspiration for a month's worth of magical freewriting, here are a few prompts and other exercises I've found especially interesting. If you use them, feel free to skip around, modify, and let your thoughts stray from the subject of the prompt as you write.

1. *I wish…* (As you do this one, watch out for limiting beliefs. Be careful not to censor your wishes before you write them down, and think of as many as you can.)

2. *A part of me would rather not think about…*

3. *I'm grateful for…*

4. *Right now I feel...* (Focus on physical sensations and, if you want, include other sensory information like what you hear and smell.)

5. Write an affirmation again and again. For example, *I am creative and magical.* See how that feels, and see if anything interesting happens afterwards.

6. Select a tarot card or random picture in a book and write *what I notice about this image is...*

7. Repeat your favorite exercise so far. Notice how it feels the same and different the second time around.

8. *One thing I really wish is...* (Follow up on the first exercise by focusing on one wish and vividly imagining what it would be like if it came true. Use a lot of sensory detail.)

9. *There are many ways my wish could come true, such as...*

10. *Thank you...for...* (Write a thank you note to a particular person or thing you appreciate.)

11. *When I think about my wish, I am afraid...* or *If I had any fear about my wish it might be...*

12. *I have a lot of habits that I rarely think about...*

13. *Last night I dreamed...* (This one sometimes takes some practice, but it's a good one to use if you do happen to remember any dreams.)

14. Take a break from journaling! Sometimes, habits stick better and longer if you feel that missing them for a single day isn't the end of the world. Or, if you really don't want to miss a day you could try something like *I've been journaling every day for the past two weeks, and so far I feel...*

15. *I may already be seeing signs that magic is at work in my life...*

16. *I'm grateful to myself for...*

17. Today, write a completely fictional diary entry. This is a great way to loosen up about the things you let yourself write and release some fear about whether they're actually true or not.

18. *I feel supported in the life I want to live when…*

19. Do a simple sketch (even if you don't really think of yourself as an artist—actually, especially if you don't really think about yourself as an artist). Then, write about how that felt and what your image looks like.

20. *There are a lot of steps I could take to move a bit closer to my wish…*

21. *A difficult thing I might be putting off doing is…*

22. Write out a question you'd like to have answered, then start writing an answer without overthinking it. Again, try not to worry about whether the answer is "true". You can get some pretty interesting answers, especially for questions of a more personal or subjective nature.

23. Today, write in a different place or position, like outside or in a coffee shop or sitting on the floor. Get a new perspective on an exercise you've already done, or just write about how this one feels.

24. *I am thinking about some things I might like to say out loud… or I would like someone to tell me…* When you're done writing, read your entry out loud. That feels kind of weird, right? Getting things down on paper is useful, but sometimes speaking them out loud can have even greater power.

25. *Recently, I've been hearing a lot about…* (Practice writing as a way to process not just your own internal state, but also other situations and ideas you encounter.)

26. *I'm ready to let go of…* or, if you're not quite sure you're ready, *I wonder if I still need to hold on to…*

27. *Something new I might like to try is…*

28. Today, write about how this month of journaling has felt. What were your favorite and least favorite exercises? Did you get any new insights into anything, or

notice any interesting shifts in your life? Do you think you'll continue this habit?

29. Repeat exercise number one, but from your current perspective. What do you really desire this month?

30. Prompt-o-matic time! You can use this set of prompt words, or create your own list out of words you love or ideas you'd like to explore. Roll a die twice to randomly select a word (for example, if you roll a 1 and a 4, use word 14). Repeat this process to choose a second word, then write about how the two concepts are alike, how they're different, how you feel about them, how they could both be involved in a story, or anything else that comes to mind.

11. desire	31. vulnerability	51. beauty
12. fear	32. work	52. sex
13. nature	33. play	53. healing
14. love	34. family	54. energy
15. conflict	35. children/childhood	55. money
16. magic	36. challenges	56. community
21. friendship	41. aging	61. gifts
22. growth	42. death	62. service
23. air	43. god/spirit	63. morality
24. earth	44. practice	64. honesty
25. water	45. art/imagery	65. boundaries
26. fire	46. coincidence	66. dreams

SPELLCASTING PART 1: GOOD INTENTIONS

The most-repeated definition of magic—though he spelled it *magick*, with a "k"—comes from Aleister Crowley. Crowley, for better or worse, may have been the most famous occultist of the 20th century. He's a very polarizing figure in the magical community, but he did have a way with words. Anyway, he said that *magick is the science and art of causing change to occur in accordance with will.*

According to this definition, we're all doing magic all the time. You're doing magic when you make a cup of tea, fill out a job application, or even read this book—you want something, and you do what you can to try to get it. Sometimes these desires (what's *in accordance with your will*) are very sharp and clear, and other times they're more amorphous. At times we get into the habit of moving through life without a lot of awareness—but in either case, your choices are moving you towards certain possibilities, and away from others. Even a lack of action is a sort of choice.

In this sense, there are also external spells at work on us all the time. We're constantly absorbing beliefs and expectations from our families and friends, the cultural environment and the random events we happen to experience. The thing that changes when you practice magic is that you start to turn this thing we're all doing all the time into an art and/or a science, which can look really different from one person to another.

For example, you could say that life hacks are a type of magic. Certainly, thinking about ways to improve your productivity (as long as they're tips that really work for you and not just a series of distractions) is a somewhat scientific way to increase your ability to cause change and achieve your goals, and we'll talk a bit more about the value and application of that type of mental technique.

Conventional self-help barely hints at the range of possibility, though. Like most of the rest of our culture, there's a huge focus on the conscious and mental aspect of personal power—which is important but hardly the whole picture. Magical techniques for increased efficacy are more likely to delve into (for example) the manipulation of energy, communication with the non-human world and tuning in to intuitive guidance, too. In most cases there are many means to an end, and the greatest flexibility of method often equates to the greatest power.

The first step to practicing any kind of magic is naming your intention. In fact, the simplest sort of spell is to state or *spell out* your intention clearly. Just doing that much can have surprising power. In some cases you will have to admit to yourself what it is that you want. In others, you might have a surprisingly tough time putting a vague feeling into words. You will have to say out loud, or write on paper (maybe both) that you really do want this thing.

I often find that this can be the hardest part of spellwork. Once you have a solid intention, the other aspects tend to come together easily. On the other hand, when a spell doesn't work, it's very often a failure of intention. It's not that you didn't want it *enough* (which is a common misconception) but more likely that you weren't correct or specific enough in your intention. I know, for example, that there are certain vague desires I've danced around for years without ever getting really clear about them. It's not that surprising that these are the situations that never really seem to move forward, magically or otherwise.

If this is your first time casting a spell, you don't have to start with a huge, earth-shaking desire. Anything that you honestly want is fine (somewhere I read, I think, about a group that practiced wishing for pie as a first intention). Once you get clear on what you actually want, you can make more plans to pursue it, using magical and material methods.

ON SPELLS THAT MIGHT BE BETTER LEFT ALONE

For most traditional Witches, no spells are entirely off limits, but there are a few types that tend to come with a lot of complications, which are probably best to avoid (at least at first). The biggest grey area is spells to help, harm or control others. While these spells might be justified in some cases, they can have a wide variety of unforeseen effects and are also unusually difficult because the people in question have their own intentions and desires. If you decide to go ahead with this kind of spell anyway, though, most of the material in this book still applies. In the case of wanting to help someone, getting their consent—or better yet, some degree of participation—is usually the most effective method as well as the highest in integrity.

Love spells are popular and can be very effective, but they're also worthy of careful consideration. The usual advice is that they shouldn't be directed toward a particular person, for exactly the reason you see in movies. Fundamentally, this is an attempt to control another person, which might destroy what attracted you to them in the first place as well as intensely complicating honest communication. On the other hand, there's a fine line between influence and control, and some people are happy enough to cast a spell on a particular person with the intention that it will only work out if it also aligns with that person's true will. The good news is, there are probably a lot more people out there with the qualities you admire, and it's much less ethically murky (as well as easier) to cast a more general magical net.

Another tricky sort of spell that tempts a lot of beginners is something along the lines of a wish for world peace. This is a common and wonderful desire, but there are two issues with starting there. The first is that wishes like this can be a sort of a cop out at times, and tend to come up when folks are resistant to naming something specific and tangible in their own lives. The second is that it's very hard to nail down the specifics. What does world peace actually look like? It's such a broad, abstract idea. If you're really feeling a powerful and personal need for peace, try to think of a way it could show up in your own life. Like the saying goes, you can start to be the peace you want to see in the world and work outward from there.

ON HOW TO SAY IT

Once you start to get a sense of what you want, there are a few steps you can take to clarify your intention. First of all, you can journal about it. Try to write freely, and don't worry about whether your first attempt to put it into words ends up going completely wrong. Write about what you might want, what you know you don't want, and how you could imagine all that working out.

As you start to get closer to an intention, write about the details of an imaginary scene, using lots of sensory detail. What might be the first sign that your wish has come true? How does it feel in your body to imagine getting that sign? What would you see, hear, feel or even smell while experiencing the thing you desire? Once you have a strong sense of a specific desire, try to put it into a single sentence. You want it to be clear and easy to say and remember, but it should also include any detail that's aimportant to you.

There are a few general conventions about good intention statements. One is that they're stated in the present tense, as though you had already received the thing you desire. Another is that they're framed in positive rather than negative terms—for example, *all my bills are paid* rather than *I don't have any debt*. The idea behind this is that you want to manifest a situation where your goal is already achieved, rather than one where you're still waiting, and that the subconscious can easily skip over little words like, "no" and pick up on the idea that you're still focused on your debt, rather than your prosperity.

Some people also like to stick a sort of disclaimer statement onto the end of their spells. There's a fear that, for example, you could cast a spell for a little extra money and end up learning that a relative died and left you an inheritance. Basically, it's a fear that the spell will work out, but in a terrible, unintended way. I think the reality behind this fear is that magical results are often surprising, and sometimes upsetting—but not usually in such a tricky, vindictive way. They can be shockingly literal at times, and I think a much more likely result of that spell for a little extra money would be to find a spare quarter in the street. Things can go wrong, like they did for Midas, but mostly if your intention is way off base or much too vague. Realistically, there's a huge difference between an intention to get some money and an intention to kill your relatives, and we are talking about intentions here. Still, if you want to tack a phrase like *...for the good of all, harming none*, or *...this or something better* onto the end of all your intention statements, you wouldn't be the first.

Most importantly, a good intention statement doesn't start out as something you believe (because of course it hasn't actually happened yet), but it should be *believable*. If you can't take your idea seriously or even imagine it happening in your life, you might want to scale back a bit. If you can't quite get yourself in line with *all my bills are already paid*, maybe try *I have a solid plan to pay my electric bill by next month*, for example. Start with something that seems possible or even likely, and see what happens. You can strengthen your belief muscles gradually.

ON RESULTS

When you've fully clarified your intention, hold it in mind for a moment then speak it out loud.

Congratulations, you've just cast a spell!

There's a lot of additional technique you can bring to this process (for example, there's a note on a popular kind of candle spell in the next section). Before we move on, though, let's talk about magical results.

People have a lot to say about what you should do next: cast more spells, don't cast any more spells for a while, work hard to make your wish come true or even forget you did it in the first place. Personally, I haven't found that forgetting is necessary, and I don't give a lot of credence to the idea that you need to create a practical way for the magic to work either. (This piece of advice goes something like: if you do a spell to get a job, you must also fill out a bunch of applications, because otherwise there's no way for the magical job to reach you.) In my experience, the result often shows up in a surprising way anyway, coming from pretty much any direction other than the path you thought you were preparing.

Most of the rest of this book is about how to increase your personal power and enhance your magical results, so there's plenty to dig into while you form your own opinions about all this. My favorite guideline for the waiting process is simple, though: do what you can to stay in a fairly constructive, optimistic and proactive state of mind. If that means walking around and filling out a bunch of job applications, great! This kind of path-smoothing is an especially good idea if there's one particular way you would prefer for the results to manifest. I think it's ok to focus on other goals, too, though, and let the details work themselves out.

For disorganized witches like myself who could end up falling in a social media hole and emerging a week later into a post-apocalyptic landscape (not the most conducive to excellent results), a simple to-do list to work on while you wait can be a surprisingly useful tool.

Remember all those other desires? What are your top five or so goals or wishes right now? This doesn't have to be a super-involved intention-setting process, just make a quick list of the ones you think you're pretty serious about. Then, go over it and notice whether there are any small steps you could take right now to move toward any of those goals. Since this is a magical list, let's say that there are no bad ideas—even silly or long-shot action steps are fine. Next, make a *short* list of the most immediate steps you'd like to try. When you've crossed those items off, go back to your big list and make another one. This should keep your magical mind constructively occupied for a while!

ON PROTECTION MAGIC

Though magic can be used for almost anything, there are a few popular kinds of spell that come up again and again—specifically, spells for love, money or prosperity, healing and protection. We'll cover one of these themes in each elemental section, beginning with protection since so many people feel a bit nervous when they're first getting started.

My most basic tip, as I mentioned before, is to stay away from it entirely if it really concerns you. There are lots of good reasons to study magic, but I've found that it isn't necessarily helpful to those who are coming to it out of a fear of curses or other malevolent forces. In most cases, those folks might be better served by some combination of therapy, spiritual practice in a tradition that feels comfortable, and possibly work with a trustworthy, experienced magical practitioner who can provide one-on-one assistance.

However, it is true that when you start to practice magic you might become more aware of the subtle energies around you, including some that feel harmful or frightening. If you're just looking to cover your bases with a little extra protection (never a bad idea), there are a few other things you could try.

First of all, if there's any sort of spirit (for example, a god or goddess, angel, animal spirit, ancestor or even just a sense of the universe as a magical force) that you feel a strong and positive connection with, you can say a simple prayer for protection and guidance every day or at least before beginning any magical work.

If you use crystals, there are a few that are known for protective properties. Jet is a good bet, because it helps to ground stray energy (including harmful vibes you could be accidentally creating yourself). Labradorite is better known for enhancing psychic energy, but it's a good pick if you'd like to strengthen your boundaries around how much of that energy you take in at the same time—plus it's really beautiful. Quartz is more of an all-purpose stone, but it's a good pick if you prefer to own just a few crystals that can be repurposed occasionally. With any stone (but especially the quartz) you can hold it and set an intention for help with a particular goal, such as protection. Then you can wear your stone, carry it in a pocket or put it in a strategic place in your home.

There are also lots of ways to work with protective boundaries. The simplest is just to spend a few minutes imagining yourself surrounded by some sort of defensive structure whenever you feel the need. You can visualize a ring or sphere of light or any other imagery that appeals to you, or work on more of a felt sense of being encircled and held by warm, protective energy. Imagine that when harmful energy comes your way, it's absorbed or reflected by the circle—but make sure to specify that non-harmful types of energy can pass through, or you may find yourself sealing off important magical channels. If you want, you can enhance this boundary work by creating a physical ring (clockwise is traditional) of salt, chalk or flower petals around your home or working area while visualizing the protective energy flowing.

If you're concerned about danger from a particular person, you can try a binding or freezing spell—take an object that symbolizes them and wrap and tie a string around it, or put it in a container of water and freeze it with the intention that that person be bound from causing you harm. Some people are quick to point out that this is technically a curse, since it's placing limits on someone else, but it's hard to think of a great argument against protecting yourself from harm.

Of course, there are other practical steps you can take toward protecting your energy, like working on your interpersonal boundaries. If a situation or conversation provokes anxiety or exhaustion, practice saying no or opting out. This is a skill that takes work (and sometimes outside support for especially challenging situations) but one that can pay off immensely with a feeling of right alignment and increased time and energy for the things you do want to grow in your life.

The next page is a coloring page designed as part of a protection spell. You can color this image in the book, copy it or download and print the file from http://lauragyre.com/creativerituals. While coloring, hold your intention for protection in mind.

CORE PRACTICE: MEDITATION

Unfortunately, most of us haven't trained our brains to focus in a way that's helpful for magical work. If we do focus intently, it's usually on something hyper-rational like a math problem. The rest of the time our mental energy can be all over the place, which isn't very helpful for anything. There are a few exceptions to this. One that's pretty familiar to a lot of people is doing creative work. You can probably remember what it's like to get really absorbed in making some kind of craft project. You could describe it as a flow state—one where you aren't constantly getting distracted, you're having a deep internal experience, and you're also able to take action in an intuitive way. That sort of focused state is one that's really useful to cultivate more of, using creative work, meditation and other similar practices.

In fact, beyond casting spells and maybe a bit of journaling, meditation is the one magical practice I would recommend to almost all Witches. There's a ton of scientific support for many of the benefits: a regular meditation practice has been shown to improve mood and overall physical health (reducing all-cause annual mortality), as well as to increase creative thinking, markers of intelligence and even productivity.

Magically speaking, basic meditation is great practice for any work involving mental focus, such as visualization or trance. There are also some more out-there studies suggesting that the energy fields of experienced meditators have a more powerful impact on the energy fields of others—so whether you want to build your own influence or work on bringing more mindful attention to the rest of the world, meditation is a good place to start. To get these benefits, regular practice is important. Some meditation is pretty much always better than none, so if you're able to set aside even five minutes a day, that's a good start. Fifteen minutes or half an hour daily will yield faster results if you can make it happen, though.

Take a minute now to close your eyes and imagine your ideal meditation environment—maybe a quiet beach at dawn, with dolphins leaping in the distance. Got it? Good. That could be an awesome intention to manifest, but let's also consider the possibility that it might be the wrong approach to meditation.

I once travelled a long way for a meditation retreat. It was an amazing experience, but the thing that really stuck with me happened at my hotel. I overheard another participant complaining (well, yelling) at great length about, ironically, noise. There was a lot of construction happening nearby, which I kind of figured was the price we paid for picking the cheapest hotel in the area.

As things went on, she got more and more self-righteous and demanding, though, sounding close to tears by the time she yelled, "But how am I supposed to do my meditation?" I'm not sure what happened after that, but I hope she figured it out, because I guess she really needed the practice—and to be fair, I sometimes feel like that myself when my kids decide to play video games in the middle of my practice time.

BUT HOW AM I SUPPOSED TO DO MY MEDITATION?

I guess the moral of the story is that you should pick the best hotel you can afford and then do your best to meditate wherever you happen to end up. At home, where you can do things however you want, you might as well pick a peaceful corner or a comfortable chair or cushion, and even set it up with things like earplugs and relaxing music or incense if they help you get in the mood. You can also experiment with time of day if your schedule is flexible, since you may find that you have an easier time first thing in the morning, as an afternoon break, or as part of your bedtime routine.

When you're ready to practice, sit comfortably with your back straight. You can use a classic cross-legged meditation posture on the edge of a cushion with your knees on the floor. If that's not workable for you, you can also sit in a chair with your back straight and feet flat on the floor. Technically, lying down can work, but there's a significant risk of falling asleep.

Tilt your head slightly forward and close your eyes or leave them open and relaxed, allowing them to lose focus. Touch the tip of your tongue to the roof of your mouth behind your front teeth (besides creating a channel for subtle energetic currents, this position will reduce the distraction of needing to swallow while practicing).

Notice your breath (magical air!) and allow it to become deep and slow, softening your belly if necessary. Focus on the sensation of the breath going in and out, maybe in a specific place like the tip of your nose. If you want, you can count a small number of breaths—say, four, or ten—then start over every time you reach that number.

That's really all there is to it, except that you will instantly start to get distracted. The entire practice of meditation is a process of gently bringing your attention back to your point of focus again and again, with as little judgment as possible over the fact that you keep getting distracted. The good news is that you don't have to do it perfectly in order to get the benefits, as long as you're willing to sit down and practice again and again. In fact, the more distractions you are (gently) fighting, the more of a concentration workout you're getting—which is a good thing to keep in mind on days when it's a real struggle, or somebody is knocking down walls in your hotel.

ON VISUALIZATION

When casting spells, it's also useful to be able to imagine the scene you wish for clearly. This is a skill you can practice! In a calm, meditative state, close your eyes and imagine any object. Visualize it in as much detail as you can. Imagine turning it around from side to side and looking at it from all angles. Try to hold on to the image exactly as you imagine it, rather than allowing your focus to drift.

You can also practice "visualizing" with different senses. For many people sight is the easiest, but if you have trouble remembering or imagining the look of things and you don't notice improvement with practice, there are plenty of workarounds. With or without a visual image, practice hearing a sound—for example, a particular voice speaking—clearly in your mind.

Regardless of which sense you're practicing, you can work your way up from a single object to a scene. Try shutting your eyes, and imagining as much of the room around you as you can. After that, try remembering something that happened to you earlier or imagining a situation that hasn't happened yet with a similar amount of detail. Eventually, practice imagining this kind of scene with as many different senses as you can.

MORE EXPERIMENTS WITH AIR

1. We'll talk about making your physical environment more magical in the next section, but there's a simple step you can take to prepare right now—just make some space. Sometimes, literally and figuratively, we have so much going on in our lives that it's hard to make room for anything else.

When I want to bring something new into my life, I try to clear out as much clutter as possible. This is good practice, even if you're not sure what it is that you want to bring in. Make the space first, and see what shows up in your life. You can take this literally (I certainly do), but you can also think a bit about other ways to make more space in your life. Is it hard to fit anything new into your weekly schedule or your social calendar? What about your closet? Is your brain stuffed full of unhelpful messages from media you don't really need to be consuming? Wherever you'd like something new to show up, make sure you have plenty of space.

2. Revise your personal rules. Remember those limiting beliefs? You may be starting to notice persistent thoughts about yourself, your future prospects and even the way the world works that you don't consciously intend or fully agree with. These internalized rules aren't as obvious as if they were posted on a sign, but they can be just as hard to avoid, and you probably follow them a lot more closely than you would prefer to.

If you don't like some of the rules you're currently operating under, consider making your own sign, changing each belief to a personal policy you like better. Your rules should be specific to your situation, but they might include things like *it's ok to want whatever I want*, or *people are allowed to believe in magic*. Make them as personal or as general as you prefer.

You could stick to using these reframed beliefs as affirmations, but if you find yourself encountering a lot of internalized rules you don't like, this sign project can be a fun and helpful way to talk to your subconscious and carve out some space on a mental as well as physical level. Make it fancy and/or official-looking, and hang it wherever you could use a reminder.

3. Hand-lettering (the process as well as the product) is also a nice way to meditate on a quote, an affirmation, or any other food for thought that you'd like to bring to mind more often. If this appeals to you, get the right materials (brushes, calligraphy pens, or even just markers) to experiment with a style you like and start practicing.

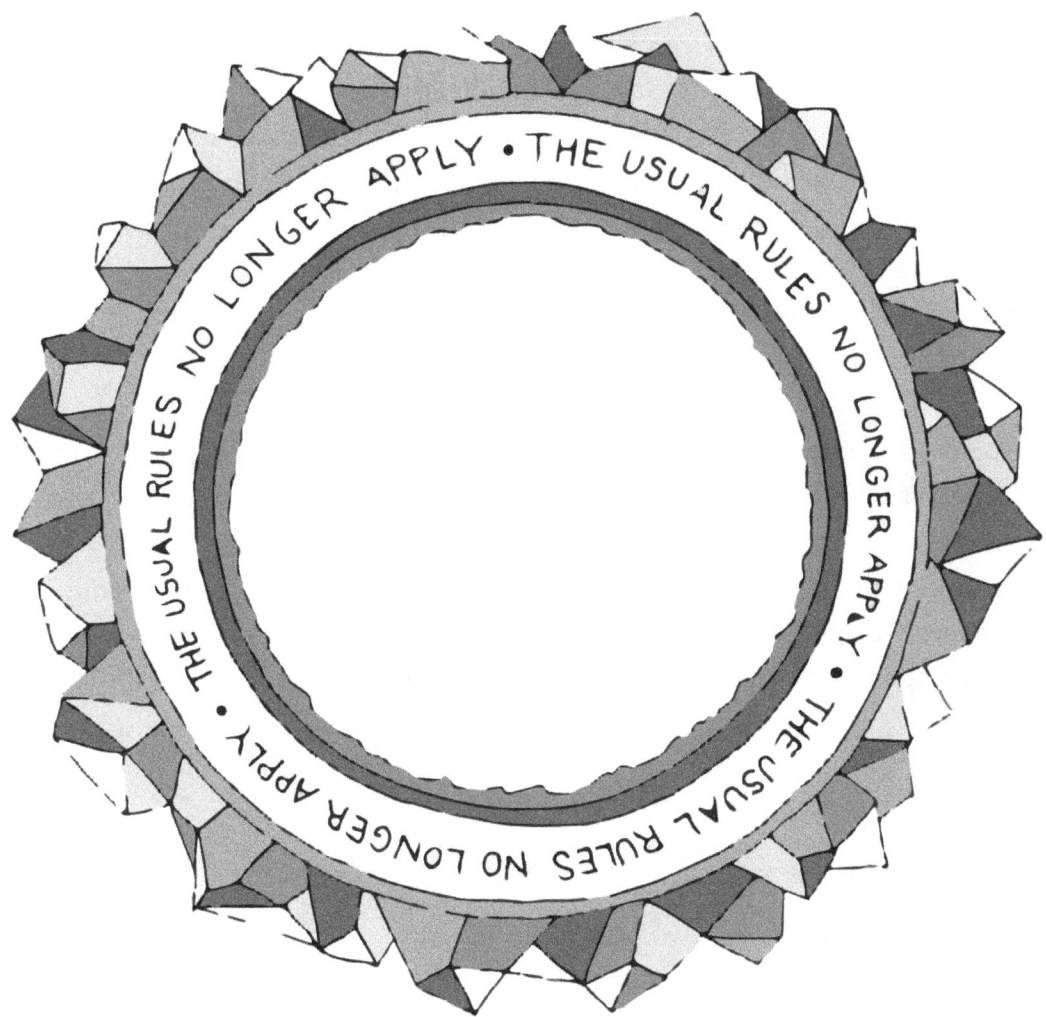

4. If you've been on the internet, you've almost certainly run into vision boards. If not, the basic idea is that you collect images that inspire you, representing things you'd like to have and do and generally the way you want to feel. Cut pictures out of magazines or find them online and print them out, then create a collage. Of course, you can also add your own drawings and decorative touches. If you spend a lot of time on a computer, you can even make a digital version to use as a screensaver. In either case, take your time with the process—you might want to spend a while collecting images before you move on to the next step, and even start a new collection for the next version once you finish the first.

Vision boards can be a fun and intuitive way to explore your desires, especially because you might find yourself attracted to images without immediately knowing why. Cutting out a bunch of things and figuring out how they fit together can be a process of self-discovery, with sometimes surprising results. Plus, like the personal rules sign, a finished vision board is a handy thing to post in a prominent place to help keep your magical priorities in mind.

5. While studying the power of air, it's all very well to work with mental, visual and goal-setting processes—but it's also good to keep that study grounded in the physical element. Air itself is all around us, but sometimes it's easy to take for granted. When you can, get into situations where you can experience it more intensely. For example, sit in an open spot outdoors on a windy day, climb to an overlook where you can see for miles, hang up a wind-chime, whistle or play a flute, fly a kite or blow some bubbles. You can think about the lessons air has to offer, but remember to let yourself relax, be in the moment and explore the airy sensations.

6. After you've spent some time with air in whatever way feels right, you could also create some art about your experience. Don't overthink it, just get out your materials (any medium) and start to play around creatively with the feeling of air in mind. You can draw on any insights that have come up in your journaling or your magical practice so far. If it's not something ephemeral, you can save this piece of art to use in the future when you want to bring more air energy into a ritual or into your life.

II. COMING DOWN TO EARTH

Earth is very important to Witches, on a number of levels. For one thing, it's where we do all of the rest of this work, so we take that pretty seriously. It's also not a place that, in general, we're eager to escape from. In many religions there's a tendency to believe that our physical experience is fundamentally full of sin, imperfect or at least kind of unreal. There are any number of unpleasant things that go along with physical existence—from pain, inconvenience and misunderstanding to violence, cruelty, destruction and death—but there are also lots of wonderful things. In fact, every wonderful thing that we're aware of is part of this earthly life. So, the path of the Witch is to try to hold those two truths at once, use magic to make the best of them, and discover what we can about their sacredness and power.

Our bodies in particular are tied to the element of earth. They're made of the same kinds of atoms as all other matter in the universe. They also allow us to have these physical experiences of feeling, seeing, hearing, smelling, tasting and influencing the material events going on around us. They are, in a way, a kind of personal crossroads where the material world meets up with the world of thought, feeling and imagination inside each of us.

Purely mental practices like those in the air section can lead to a lot of internal freedom, an increased sense of focus and greater personal wellbeing. Mental practice alone is rarely enough to manifest much change in the physical world, though. In order to move forward, we need to bring movement, sensation and physical matter into the work. In this section we'll explore some ways to bring more enchantment into your daily life and more practical action into your magic, eventually combining the two to manifest the material changes you desire.

ON THE BODY AS A MAGICAL TOOL

The body is an important tool for magic. There's a lot to consider there, from the impact of magic on our physical and mental health (and, conversely, of our physical and mental health on our magic) to the idea of a sort of spiritual or energetic layer of the body that we can strengthen, expand and use for magical purposes.

Before we get too far into that theory, though, take a minute to get centered in your body right now. Adjust anything that needs adjusting to make yourself as comfortable as possible, then take a couple of deep breaths. Notice, especially, the way that your weight sinks down and your body is supported by the ground or whatever you're resting on. Scan your body quickly for any particular sensation you might be experiencing. Cold? Thirst? The texture of a surface you're touching? Even comfort can be a noticeable sensation, though one that we tend to ignore a lot of the time.

Missing this kind of minor sensation isn't inevitable, but it is pretty culturally normal. Most of us have been socialized to ignore our physical impulses in favor of structured and mental activity (long hours of sitting still at a desk, for example). To some extent this kind of socialization is a natural process, but most of us could stand to unlearn it a little. Even if you're not going to act on every sensation you notice, being aware of more of them as they pass by will give you a greater understanding of your overall state. For example, you might not notice that you're a bit hungry until you also get mad about some minor inconvenience. Wouldn't it be great to head that process off by tuning in to that sensation of hunger in time to get a snack?

Magically speaking, you're also much more likely to actualize your desires when you're consciously aware of what those desires are, and some of those desires (maybe all of them, on some level) live in your body.

ON KNOWING IN YOUR GUT

For example, did you know that the largest collection of neurons outside the brain is located in the intestines? In this sense, having a gut feeling about something makes a lot of sense. The gut is a good place to check for information showing up in an intuitive, non-rational way.

Here's a trick to tune in to your body wisdom quickly, which I got from Martha Beck's work and use a lot. Close your eyes (if you want) and pay attention to exactly how your right hand feels. You don't need to describe it, just pay attention to the sensations. Then, switch to your left hand and vividly experience how it's feeling right now. When you've got that, try to pay attention to both at once. That's a little overwhelming, and so it helps you tune in with your whole mind quickly.

You know that idea about how the left side of your brain is rational and the right side is intuitive? That's actually been debunked somewhat on a scientific level, but it's a powerful image, and there is some evidence that physical involvement across the midline of the body helps to engage the whole brain in a healthy way. I sometimes wonder if the standard palms-together prayer posture is so popular because it unconsciously triggers this kind of bilateral body-mind engagement.

In any case, once you run through those steps you'll probably feel a bit calmer and more aware of your body. Let that awareness sink into your belly, a couple of inches below the belly button, and check for sensations there. If you feel them, you'll probably be able to guess what they mean. A little bit of nervous tension can actually be a good thing, especially if accompanied by a feeling of excitement or curiosity. On the other hand, if what you feel is more like dullness or even dread, that's a pretty clear referendum on something that's going on from your body. Getting more information might change your gut feeling, of course, but often your body can pick up important information that you're not even aware of on a conscious level.

CORE PRACTICE: FEELING ENERGY

Another cool thing about the human body is that besides the wheel of elements, it might be the most common cross-cultural magical map. Energy flows throughout the body in a way that generally reflects the shape of the physical body, but there are specific parts of the body where certain types of energy tend to accumulate. The chakra system is probably the best-known version of this map, consisting of seven or eight energy centers rising from the base of the spine to the top of the head, each with its own qualities (for example, the heart chakra is associated with feelings of love and compassion) and, to some extent, mapped near glands that have related physical functions in the body.

The chakra map comes from India, but most of us encounter it in a form that bears little resemblance to the original — for example, there are far more than seven traditional chakras, and none of them are arranged in rainbow order. However, the basic concept of these energetic centers, located mainly along the midline of the body, is fairly universal. Chinese, Greek and Celtic lore place an emphasis on three main centers, in the head, lower belly and heart, and this is a model that a lot of us seem to be able to connect with intuitively.

The mental work we did in the air section (particularly meditation) strengthens the heavenly, transcendent energy of the head center. The belly center, on the other hand, is associated with earthier physical energies ranging from hunger and sexual sensation to fear and all kinds of instinctive gut feeling. When we can get these two types of energy working in harmony, our personal power increases and the heart center, where they meet and hopefully achieve some kind of balance, is also strengthened.

If this kind of talk about energy is new to you, the easiest way to understand it is probably to try some experiments. First of all, sit or stand comfortably, take a few deep breaths and start to focus on sensation in your body.

Raise your hands and notice how they feel. Now, rub them together briskly. They might start to tingle or feel warmer. This is a natural result of friction, but it's *also* a way to increase your sensitivity to subtle energy. Bring your hands apart, then slowly back toward each other. Move your hands together and apart, feeling for any interesting sensations. People who try this exercise often report additional feelings of tingling or light pressure at a certain point, like the feeling of pushing weak magnets together while they repel each other. You might be able to feel this energy in layers, maybe when your hands are about a foot apart, and again when they're close to touching. Sometimes, moving back and forth through this energy field can feel a bit like pulling taffy, stretching something as your hands move apart, then compressing it as they come together again. You can use these sensations to feel that you're building up a ball of energy in your hands.

When you can feel that, try playing with the ball—making it bigger and smaller, and moving it around. You can also pass it over other parts of your body and see how that feels. Sometimes it can feel soothing or energizing, which is how simple energy medicine works (try this when you have some sort of physical symptom, and see what happens).

When you're done experimenting, your energy body should settle back into its normal pattern fairly quickly. If you're left with any uncomfortable sensations you can put your palms on the ground to release any lingering loose energy.

ON THE WORD *ENERGY*

One of the complicated things about magic is that the terminology can be really hard to pin down. Talk about the spiritual energy that flows through and around the body is common, but what does it really mean? There are many types of energy present in the human body, from heat energy to the electromagnetic waves generated by the brain and heart. These energies do pass through our bodies in certain perceptible ways, fluctuating based on our actions, feelings and thought-patterns—and there is solid evidence that we can train to have more conscious control over these energies and thus more influence on the world around us on a subtle level. However, this is a field that science is just starting to make sense of, and in many cases magical practitioners are basing their work on centuries of tradition that have used these words in a meaningful but not exactly scientific sense. So, I'll continue to use the word *energy* loosely, to mean something like a *sense of something subtle and changeable, possibly associated with particular qualities that may be present in or move through a space.* For example, you could say that a room has a pleasant energy if walking into it makes you feel good for reasons (which might or might not have anything to do with electromagnetic frequencies) that seem unrelated to obvious features like the style of decoration. A sense of energy passing through a part of the body probably has something to do with subtle electromagnetic charges, but even more to do with the expansion of blood vessels and an increase in warmth that can come with the right kind of attention. In general, this language often seems to be a shorthand for the aggregate of a million little factors that are too small to perceive consciously, but that our intuitive minds are willing to keep tabs on and sum up for us as energy. *Awen*, the Welsh word for a similar concept comes from the words for *flowing essence*, which I think is particularly poetic.

MORE EXPERIMENTS WITH ENERGY

If you want to experiment more, you can try these exercises with a friend. Make an energy ball. Have them make one, too, to get a feeling for how this works. Squish them together. Push it towards them, then pull it toward yourself. Have them try that, and see how it feels. Try passing the balls back and forth. How big can you make one by moving away from each other? What about passing them over each other's bodies, to see how that feels?

People (and animals) have pretty strong energy fields, so they're good to practice with. Close your eyes and ask a friend to stand quietly somewhere in a large room or outdoors. Make an energy ball to tune in to this feeling, then hold your hands up in front of you, palms facing forward. Walk around slowly, feeling for subtle changes in energy sensation. Can you figure out where your friend is before you run into them?

If you can, try it with trees or other plants. Try it outside in an open field—turn around with your eyes closed, palms facing out, and see if the energy feels different in any direction. Try it in a few different places. Can you guess which direction is north (I often can, but if you're in the Southern Hemisphere maybe you will feel south more strongly)?

Another thing you can try with a friend is to practice projecting energy or turning it off (actually, you can't really turn it off, but you can dampen it somewhat). One person sits down in front of the other. The second stands, placing their hands over the first person's head, palms down (the crown of the head is often a high-powered energy location).

The seated person should drop into a meditative state, imagining themselves filling up with so much energy that it starts to pour out of the top of their head. If the standing person can feel that, the sitter could try deciding to project energy or, alternately, imagining that the energy goes away and the top of their head is covered with cold mashed potatoes (I believe I may have learned this mashed potato trick from a Robert Anton Wilson book; it's weirdly effective). The stander can see whether they can guess when the sitter is projecting vs. potatoing their energy.

Some people can also see this sort of energy. Have your partner (or, in a pinch, pet or potted plant) stand in front of a white wall while practicing energy exercises. Let your eyes unfocus a bit, watching them. See if you can perceive any change in appearance, such as a faint color or blurring around their body.

And then, of course, there are more subtle, less localized types of energy. Pay attention to how the energy feels when you walk into a new space. When you wake up in the morning, check in with your own energy, too. Do you feel energetic, or kind of low? Creative, cozy, emotionally fragile, ready to work hard? This isn't exactly the same kind of energy that we usually practice manipulating, but there are a lot of subtle currents along similar lines that are worth tuning in to more closely—and you never know, you might learn to move them around, too.

ON NOT FEELING IT

If you try this kind of exercise and don't feel anything, the significance of that is not necessarily much. For one thing, this may be an entirely new skill set for you, and new skills take practice. I would try it a number of times before deciding that it isn't going to happen. You could also work with other earth practices to get more comfortable with and mindful of physical sensation in general.

If you think you might feel something but you're not sure if you're imagining it, that totally counts! A lot of magical skills exist right there on the threshold of the physical and the imagination. Whatever you think you feel, work with that. The sensation will probably get more vivid over time. On the other hand, it's possible that you won't feel anything at all. Different people have different skills, and that seems to go at least double for magic. Some people are great at visualization and others aren't, and some people may never really have a physically felt experience of magical energy.

If that's you, it probably just means you have a different set of magical abilities. Maybe your dreams will tend to come true, your spells will work extra well, you'll perceive intuitive information through daydream scenarios, or you'll make astoundingly effective magical tools. Don't rule out the possibility that your aptitudes may change in the future, but try not to worry about it either. Be honest about what you can and can't do—especially with yourself—and remember to focus on your strengths as well as your weaknesses.

ON PHYSICAL MOVEMENT AND EXERCISE

This can be a touchy subject (ha), but I want to briefly mention some thoughts about movement and magic. In general, physical exercise is conducive to optimal physical ability (whatever that looks like for you), an improved sense of empowerment and wellbeing and also a direct experience of being in touch with your body. This, in turn, can increase your elemental earth power and your personal sense of wholeness.

The type of movement isn't too important. Yoga and some traditional martial arts are popular and might have special benefits, because they were developed by people who were aware of the subtle energetic currents of the body. So, they can sometimes do double-duty as exercise and energetic practice, especially with a teacher who's informed about those dimensions. If you do decide to try something along those lines for the first time, shop around a little before committing to a particular practice, because different forms and teaching styles vary widely. An in-person class can be a great experience and help with nuance, community and accountability, but there are also a lot of great videos available online if you're more comfortable practicing at home or if money is an issue.

If those sorts of movement aren't your thing, traditional exercise from weight training to aerobics can still do a lot for your sense of personal power and physical awareness. And, of course, there's a special benefit to any exercise you get while doing something you love (like dancing or skiing) or anything outdoors that can get you in closer touch with the earth itself while you move. Even gentle, mindful walking on a regular basis is a great plan if that's what your body is up for.

As great as exercise can be, though, it's a thing we have a lot of cultural shaming around—especially as it relates to body image—and there's nothing very magical about that. You don't have to love every minute of your movement program, but if there's no way you can mostly enjoy or appreciate it, please don't think that you have some kind of moral or Witchcraft-based obligation to exercise anyway. The actual point is that you don't have to do anything you don't want to!

If you choose not to exercise, though, maybe think a bit about whether there's another way to connect with your body that might feel better. Can you get a massage? What about taking a hot bath with some magical herbs? There's actually some evidence that heating your body like that has a lot of the same physical benefits as exercise—so if you

feel like you need an excuse, I hope that helps.

ON FEELINGS

In some elemental maps, emotions are associated most strongly with the realm of water, but I don't like that placement very much. This is because, fundamentally, body sensations are a part of earth, and feelings are what we experience when our bodies respond to thoughts.

For example, a particular thought might make you clench your jaw and maybe your fists, feel a painful hollowness in your chest or stomach, smile to yourself, notice an electrical sensation throughout your body, or even start to cry. Less intense feelings are also taking place in the body, though the sensations might be more subtle. Sometimes, a physical feeling of happiness is just a relaxing sense of other less comfortable states draining away.

Next time you have an emotional response to something, check in with your felt sensations. If you don't notice a physical dimension at first, look for the feeling in your body. Where do you feel it most strongly? Even if you have to use your imagination to locate it somewhere in the map of your body, where would that be? What does the emotion feel like? Cold or warm? Pleasant or painful? What shape is it? Does the feeling change or move from place to place?

When you start to observe your feelings in terms of physical sensation, you don't necessarily have to do anything else about them. Feelings are never the enemy, and just being fully aware of them is often helpful! However, you might find (especially for uncomfortable feelings) that you naturally start to relax the muscles involved, which can also help to release unwanted emotions, loosen the thought-patterns that trigger them, and even free you up to approach the situations causing the feelings in a calmer, more constructive state of mind.

This is almost the opposite of how we often expect to deal with emotional issues, but it really does work in a lot of day-to-day situations. This is because communication with the body is a two-way street. The thoughts we think and the things we experience lead to certain physical states, but changing physical states can also lead pretty directly back to different thoughts and actions. This is an incredibly powerful feedback loop, and one that's well worth developing some conscious awareness around.

ON TRAUMA AND MAGIC

Even typical, every-day feelings have a powerful effect on our physical function, but some experiences have a greater and longer-lasting effect. In particular, any experience that causes trauma tends to have a lasting impact on the body. The roots of this can be the sort of things that we usually consider traumatic, such as violence and serious accidents, but they can also include less extreme shocks and scares. Even chronic, unavoidable stress or intimate involvement with someone else's trauma can lead to post-traumatic patterns in the body and mind. This is not to say that all these types of trauma are equivalent, because they're certainly not. But there's a definition of trauma as any experience that overwhelms our ability to cope, and when you put it that way it's something that most of us can relate to in some way.

When we're not traumatized, our nervous systems work to balance excitement and relaxation. If something scary happens, the sympathetic nervous system takes over temporarily, producing hormones like adrenaline that help us focus and prepare to run or fight if necessary. When the danger has passed, the parasympathetic nervous system kicks back in and allows us to relax in order to rest, digest, and do the variety of other things we do in our daily lives. If the danger is too overwhelming, too repetitive or lasts for too long, we can get stuck in reactive sympathetic nervous system loops. Although these feelings can be triggered by thoughts or events that remind us of the original trauma, they're not fundamentally caused by the thoughts—they're caused by a nervous system that has forgotten how to relax.

How does all that relate to Witchcraft? There are a few connections that I think are worth considering. First of all, I want to acknowledge that this can be a significant issue and suggest that you be aware of your own trauma history when taking on any practices that might feel uncomfortable to you. There are lots of ways to work with emotion that are really great for dealing with common situations, but not so great if you find them so triggering that you tend to feel overwhelmed all over again. Challenging yourself is a good thing, but so is knowing your limits—and skipping a practice today doesn't mean that it will never work for you in the future.

On the other hand, though, many people find that an appropriate magical practice can help reduce the ongoing impact of trauma in their lives over time. In fact, a case could be made that a lot of types of religious and spiritual practice (when properly applied, in a way that doesn't make people feel worse about themselves) have a major function of releasing trauma, which is pretty useful on an individual and community level when there's so much of it going around.

This is particularly true for practices with an ecstatic or physical dimension. Witches and massage therapists have long been saying that emotional pain can get stored in the body. This means that when you have a traumatic experience it can cause ongoing physical symptoms like tightness in certain muscles, and also (again, that feedback loop that works in both directions) when that muscle tightness is relieved you may experience an emotional reaction and usually some relief around thoughts of the event that caused the tension to get stored. This is why, for example, people sometimes burst into tears while doing yoga but then feel better afterwards.

Science has been catching up with this kind of thinking recently, leading to some really interesting developments. For example, psychological researcher Peter Levine studied wild animals, who are exposed to life threatening situations on a regular basis, to see how they deal with trauma. He noticed that when animals were unable to escape from a dangerous situation they tended to freeze up or go limp, but then when the danger had passed their bodies would start to shake uncontrollably. He believes (and many trauma specialists now agree) that this period of physical release is important to healthy integration of intense experience, and can't be replaced by mental processing alone.

Unfortunately, this kind of shaking is something that we humans don't tend to do naturally (or, rather, if it starts to happen naturally we may decide that it looks weird or feels scary, and make it stop). We do have a remarkable cross-cultural tendency to come up with rituals that involve shaking, though! Many of them are quite complicated and culturally specific, but even dancing freely can sometimes serve a similar function. If you don't participate in any traditional forms of shaking, you might want to check out what modern somatic (body-based) therapy has to offer. Dr. David Bercelli has developed a set of trauma releasing exercises (also called TRE) based on natural shaking movements for the particular purpose of teaching in large groups and to people who don't necessarily have professional support. There are lots of videos available if this is something you'd like to experiment with, and of course there are lots of experts from somatic psychologists to yoga teachers and massage therapists who can provide personal support for trauma in the body if that's something you could use.

I hope this information is helpful if you know that you're dealing with a history of trauma, but I also think that low-level trauma is an important consideration on the magical path in general. One of the big things that often gets in the way of *change in accordance with our wills* is a stew of emotional patterns and habits from the past. These patterns aren't usually very useful in achieving our current goals, they can muddy our natural intuition, and in many cases they're lingering results of (often) low-level trauma that we may not even be aware of. Unravelling this stuff is an ongoing process that is never really going to be finished (one of those consequences of living in the material world). The more of it that we're able to release, though, the more of our energy and power we can free up to proactively go after the things we want right now, and the more present we can be with others as they deal with similar struggles.

ON THE POWER OF THE EARTH ITSELF

Of course, the earth itself is also an important part of earth magic. Our bodies and every other aspect of our beings evolved in an environment, or rather a wide variety of environments that share some things in common. So did ancient human cultures, and by the time Witchcraft was on the scene the nature situation wasn't all that different. Of course, we don't and shouldn't practice Witchcraft exactly the same way that our ancestors did, and there's nothing wrong with a little techno-paganism if that's your thing. There are many magical lessons to learn from immersion in nature, though, from sensory awareness, embodied experience and the interconnection of all things to the gifts of individual plants, animals and powerful places. Plus, spending time in nature is usually great for our physical and mental health, and tends to have a naturally positive influence on our state of elemental balance.

These are, fundamentally, lessons and benefits that can't come from a book. So, I guess this is just to say that, yes, spending time with nature totally counts as magical practice. Go for a walk, visit a new park, watch nature documentaries, learn about traditional crafts using natural materials, make art about plants and animals, meditate outside and experience the changing seasons.

The seasons, in particular, have a lot to teach about patience and working along with your environment rather than fighting against it. One of the bits of Wiccan lore that I still tend to use (though I do use it a bit loosely) is called the Wheel of the Year. This is a calendar with a set of eight seasonal holidays that some Witches use to tune in to what's going on in the natural world. It was cobbled together from a variety of European cultural practices, plus apparently some stuff that folks just felt like adding...but it does reflect the fact that many traditional cultures do observe the solstices and equinoxes, and significant cultural activities tend to happen around the other four holidays (sometimes called the cross-quarter days).

Here's a quick summary of some highlights of these holidays, in case you could use more things to celebrate:

A holiday that might be called Halloween or All Hallows' Eve or Samhain comes around the end of October. Many Witches consider this to be the spiritual new year, though I prefer to think of it as the end of the old year which is followed by a pause. A nice feature of this holiday cycle is a dark, fallow period between this day and the Winter Solstice, coming at a time of year when a lot of us could use some extra quiet and rest. A traditional time of year for slaughtering animals before winter, themes of death, spooky shadow stuff and ancestor veneration. Apple cider and trick-or-treating have traditional roots, too!

A holiday that might be called Yule or the Winter Solstice is astronomically determined to be around December 21 (or, June 21st in the Southern hemisphere...generally Witches invert the entire calendar as needed, since the holidays have such a seasonal basis). If Halloween was the death of the old year, this is the birth of the new year along with the sun. This is also the shortest day of the year and the turning point after which the days start to get longer, and several solar-aligned gods celebrate their births around this time of year. It's a time for staying cozy and festive with family and friends, warming spices, fire in the fireplace and generous gifts.

A holiday that might be called Imbolc, Candlemass or Groundhog's Day comes around the beginning of February. Though it might be even colder than it was in December, the sun that was reborn at Yule is already growing stronger and the lengthening days are starting to be felt in a very real way. It's also a time of year when the days of cold and restricted movement can start to feel a bit endless, so it's a good time to light (or even make) some candles and look forward with hope. Traditional foods reflect the fact that the first farm animals might start to give birth and make milk around this time of year—possibly the first fresh food of the new year after a difficult winter. Besides obvious dairy foods, rich pancakes and pastries are common.

A holiday that might be called Ostara or the Spring Equinox falls around March 21st. This is a good time to think about new beginnings and start preparing for the summer more seriously by spring cleaning, planting seedlings indoors and hopefully enjoying a few warm afternoons outside. Eggs and fresh greens are popular foods. There's often quite a bit of cultural overlap between pagan and non-pagan holidays, but the Easter season is a particularly striking example. Fertility symbols like rabbits and eggs make a lot more sense in a witchy context, so you can totally get away with making Ostara eggs if you want to.

A holiday that is overwhelmingly called May Day falls on May 1. Like Halloween, this holiday has significantly persisted in popular culture. Besides the magic of the season of warm weather, blooming flowers and the generally explosive fertility of nature, May Day has also become a workers' holiday, celebrating the power of the community and the importance of taking a day off. In many places, you can find parties, marches and maypole dances. Traditional activities also include spending a night out in the woods and surprising friends with wildflowers. No particular stand-out foods (chocolate? I don't know if it's traditional, but it seems appropriately indulgent), but it's a great time for feasting and drinking, too.

A holiday called Midsummer (confusing at the beginning of the calendar-based summer, but it is the astrological middle of the summer) or the Summer Solstice falls around June 21. There's relatively little lore about this day because I assume people are too busy swimming, stuffing themselves at picnics and generally enjoying a relaxing time of the year. It is said to be a good day for spotting fairies, though, and harvesting magical herbs. There's also a slightly bittersweet note, because at the height of summer we start looking toward darker days and the death of the year.

A holiday sometimes called Lammas or Lughnasadh comes around the beginning of August. This is the first of three harvest festivals, specifically celebrating the beginning of the grain harvest. Bread baking, beer, and bonfires are popular. It's also worth considering the slow, dragging feeling that tends to set in around this time of year, almost like it does in February. How long will it be this hot? Isn't school going to start again soon? It's not an especially popular time of year, but it does have its own magic and lessons if you can tune in and take it slowly.

A holiday sometimes called Mabon or the Autumn Equinox is astronomically determined and falls around September 21st. In the middle of the harvest season, this used to be a time to process and put away food. It's also a fairly low-intensity holiday, but a good time to make some soup and jam and think about what you need to do to organize your life and your projects through the next inward-turning cold season.

Whether you adopt some or all of these holidays or continue to use a different calendar, observing the turning of the year with seasonal food, decoration, time outside, celebration and community is a great way of tapping into the energy of earth.

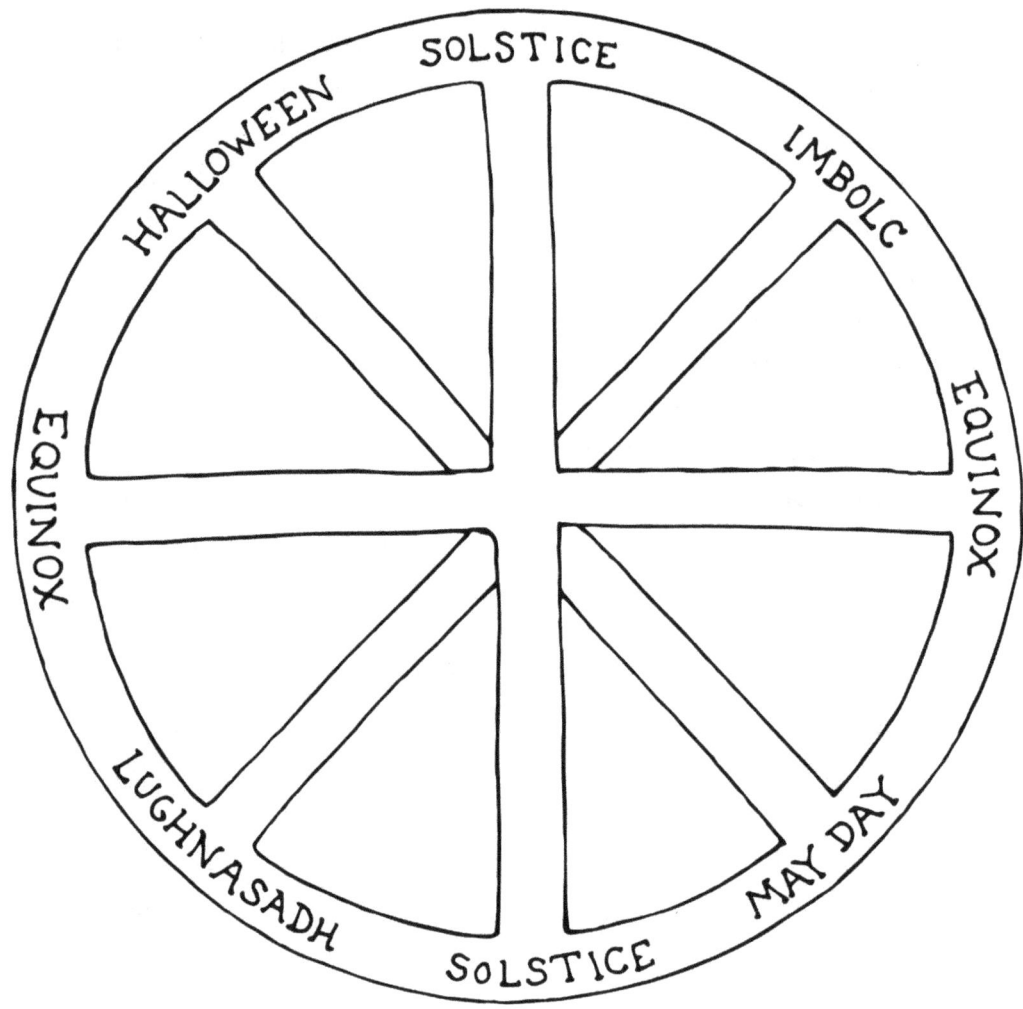

ON MAGICAL SPACE

There's one more earthy thing we should probably talk about for a minute, which is the physical space you spend your time in. How well does it support you in living a healthy, happy, magical life? This is probably your home, but it could also apply to your workplace or even a car you spend a lot of time in. These places are bigger than us, literally and figuratively, and in many ways outside of our control. Hopefully you like your home well enough, but even if you do there might be some environmental issues that are hard to avoid. You might live with others, and certainly your control over your environment at work is probably limited.

On the other hand, there are probably plenty of ways that you can and do influence your environment, and the way that you maintain your space and your belongings might be the biggest one. At the risk of generalizing too much, this is something that isn't...

an incredibly strong point for a lot of witchy folks, myself included. Quick, which feels more exciting and magical—reading a new book for inspiration, or washing your dishes? This isn't about perfection. There's no barrier to entry for Witchcraft. If your life is busy and stressful, you have trouble staying organized or you never seem to get around to the cleaning you have planned, you can still get a lot out of magic.

Many of us seem to have a weird mental block around this stuff, though. We'll think and talk about our magical goals as though we'd do anything to accomplish them, but would we really? It's sometimes hard to believe in that kind of thing when you have trouble following through with even basic tasks. So, here's another question: which feels more magical—casting a spell as a pile of your stuff is creeping across all your floors, or casting it in a space that you spent a doable amount of time tidying and preparing? Also, what would it be like to wake up in a place where you feel comfortable and inspired to do work like that every day? Is that one of your magical goals, and if so are you taking it seriously?

Cleaning can be a big issue for a lot of us, but I'm not *just* talking about cleaning. The earth stuff you need to deal with might be a mountain of paperwork, or a long to-do list for work that keeps getting longer and threatening to swamp you. And just to be crystal clear, none of this is a referendum on your value—you're great (and magical) the way you are! It's normal to have tasks that you find hard to deal with; pretty much all of us do, regardless of what social media might seem to indicate. All I'm suggesting is that we think of these earthly challenges (whatever they might be) as part of our magical practice, rather than a distraction that exists in some sort of alternate dimension.

For what it's worth, this issue may also relate to elemental balance. Many of us are more willing to think adventurously, dream adventurously, and stretch outside of our overall comfort zones than we are to adventurously take on the daily, physical tasks that earthly life requires. There are exceptions, but many spiritual folks are dangerously earth-deficient. This would be ironic on what could be called a path of earth spirituality, except that it's probably no accident. We're desperate to bring more of this earth energy into our lives, but would prefer to find a workaround, some kind of *magical* fix.

Unfortunately, as occult writer Jason Miller says, *there is no magic magic.*

Which is to say, there's plenty of magic, and it's extremely magical. But, there's no magic so magical that you won't have to confront and deal with the specific personal issues that are holding you back. That's actually the opposite of how it works, more or less.

If you do magic in an escapist way, you might get some results, but they're more likely to be escapist results. The more you head straight toward the challenges (yes, all the challenges) and integrate magic into your entire life, the more that effort and integration will be reflected in your results.

I know—sorry about that.

So, what about picking one project or habit that would feel really good to see some movement on? Does it need to be broken down into manageable daily or weekly tasks? What if you took that on as a part of your magical practice? Err on the side of starting small because, again, we can build more confidence as we see it happening.

A FEW MORE NOTES ON HOUSEWORK

First of all, keep in mind that you can think of all the housework you do as spiritual practice. It counts! As you mop and sort stuff, imagine the feelings that you would like to experience and maybe share with others in your space. More calm, more comfort, more excitement, more creativity, more love? With intention, you can invite these feelings into your space as you go. You can also dedicate your work as a devotional offering to the universe, a particular spirit, a spell you're working on or your highest self (your future self will surely appreciate your efforts, too).

You can also try to switch up your energy in a sensory way. If it helps to set the mood, listen to inspiring music or spiritual podcasts or a funny audiobook while you work. Build in breaks, and rest or do something fun for a few minutes when your energy gets too low. Personally, I like to make check-lists with lots of little items. Checking things off is fun! You accomplished something!

If you make your own cleaning products, include some herbs corresponding to your intentions, or buy a magical floor wash (lots of kinds are available). Burn some incense or aromatic herbs (I love mugwort, personally) or spray some essential oil if you like that sort of thing. As the smell fills your space, visualize things getting clean on an energetic as well as physical level. Finish by sweeping, and sweep the stagnant energy out the front door. We don't have all these brooms for nothing!

You know the feeling of lightness that happens in a newly-cleaned space? Once it happens, that particular shift in energy is pretty hard to ignore. And, of course, there are a lot of related, equally refreshing feelings, like the feeling of finally getting those emails dealt with, or getting to the bottom of your to-do list. These things are certainly not a prerequisite for doing magic, but getting them done can provide a significant boost to your wellbeing and your mental focus, as well as moving you closer to your other goals.

ON HOUSEHOLD CHARMS

Once again, and especially until you develop more ongoing rituals of your own, this is a place to lean heavily on what *feels* magical to you. But, there are a few common places to start, like bringing some natural things into your space: seasonal flowers, leaves or branches, feathers and so on. Stones are good, especially if you found them somewhere interesting. Crystals are popular, famous for their magical properties and I'll admit that I own a few. It's worth keeping in mind that many crystals are mined in ecologically devastating ways, though, and there are certainly plenty of highly magical alternatives.

Art is almost always good. Hang up some of your own, or some that inspires you. Play some music, if you aren't already in the habit. Keep some books around that you actually like, rather than just the ones you feel like you should be reading.

And, remember that suggestion about dressing for the job you want, not the job you have? There are all kinds of cartoons about people showing up to work in superhero costumes and so on, which is silly but not a bad idea if you can get away with it. Your stylistic choices are important because you carry them around all the time, not just when you're at home. It doesn't have to be a superhero outfit, but anything that makes you feel more magical is a good bet, whether that means a suit or a mystical robe. Some people like to buy a piece of jewelry (there are plenty with Witchcraft themes) or just pick something they own that already feels magical to wear as a reminder of their spiritual goals. You can also slip a special stone or similar item in your pocket or bag to carry around with you all day in a less conspicuous way.

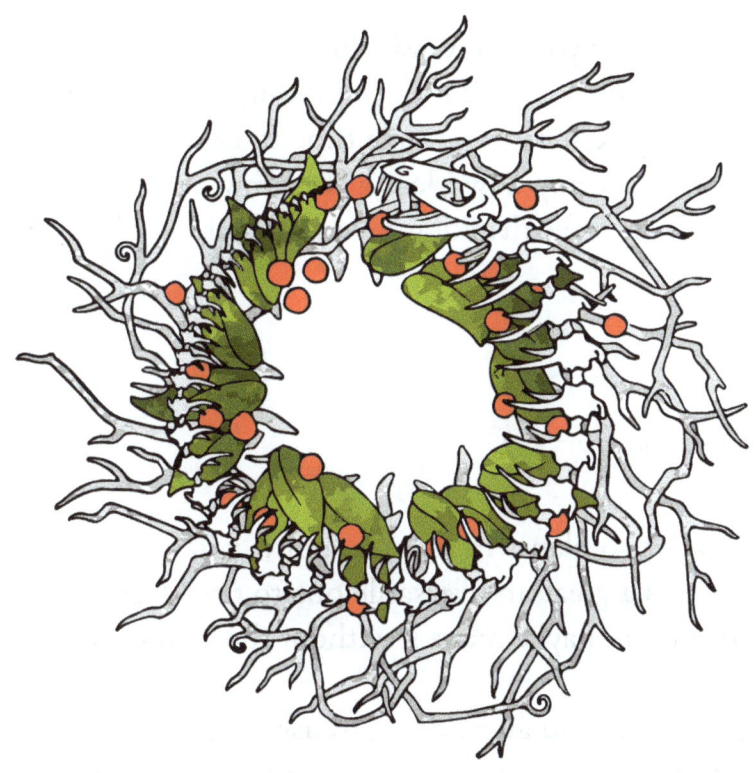

ON KITCHEN WITCHERY

Cooking is another classic witchy activity, often mentioned in stories. Witches are particularly known for their cauldrons, cooking knives, gardens and magical herbs. Herbs especially are a deep, deep area of inquiry that we'll only be able to skim the surface of here, but if you want to learn more about incorporating herbs into your practice, you're certainly in good company.

Herb magic is also a good example of how the elemental model itself is fractal, meaning that things can be broken down based on their elemental qualities at a number of different levels. On one level, it's easy to say that all herbs are earth magic because they grow naturally out of the ground, but it's also true that some herbs are considered to have a *more* earthy nature than others, while others are earthy but also more airy, watery or firey than other herbs. In fact, if you're attracted to herbal magic you can look into energetics and use herbs as one method of adjusting your elemental balance. (In particular, look for resources that mention traditional Western herbalism, which is based on this four-element system).

One thing you can easily try with little guidance is picking out an herbal tea (start with a single herb or plant, if you really want to get to know it—the ginger tea below would be a fine choice, even though it isn't technically an herb) and drink it regularly. The effects of most herbs are subtle and take time to develop, so ask yourself whether you feel any different or have any new ideas after a few days, a week or even a month. You can also do a gut check while drinking a cup to see if your body has any immediate feedback.

GINGER LEMON HONEY TEA

Technically there are two plants in this tea, but if you want to have a single herbal remedy in your life this is a great and versatile one to try. Drink it if you have a cold, a sore throat or a headache, or maybe make it without the lemon if your stomach is upset.

Buy a fresh ginger root. If you aren't going to use it right away, store it in the freezer. When you're ready, grate at least a teaspoon of ginger (use the extra fine side of a grater, or a microplane to easily grate frozen ginger). Bring at least a cup of water to a boil, add the ginger and steep for a few minutes, then pour through a strainer or coffee filter, and don't worry if a little ginger gets through.

Stir in lemon and honey to taste, then drink hot or cool down to drink later. Raw local honey, by the way, is also a healing superfood with an impressive history, from mead-making to medicinal use as an antiseptic and a defense against seasonal pollen allergies.

You can also experiment with the energetic effects of your food choices. Obviously, there's no one way that Witches eat. For example, some people prefer a vegan or vegetarian diet for ethical reasons, or because they feel clearer and more intuitive when they avoid animal products. Others find it meaningful to participate directly in a food chain involving animals, or feel more grounded and nourished when they eat animal foods. Then, of course, there are also emotional and cultural associations. Most of us feel fed on an emotional level when we eat foods that we associate with festive occasions and happy memories.

Most of us can also agree that fresh plant foods (whether combined with animal products or not) are deeply nourishing, potentially delicious, and a good way to get in touch with natural processes that we're often somewhat alienated from. So, here are a few simple recipe templates that I like to use often. I offer them here primarily as a starting point—they probably won't be of much use to experienced cooks, but if you haven't cooked a lot or thought much about your food choices, I hope they'll encourage you to give it a try and see whether you don't feel a deeper connection to the earth and even to your own body.

In the case of food, listening to your body is especially important. Food can have a profound effect on us, but it's also highly individual. According to most traditional systems of healing, different foods are best for different people because of our different constitutions and life circumstances. So, if these plant-based ideas appeal to you, there's plenty you can do in this direction. For example, you could focus more on local, seasonal foods. That's a great way to get more involved in your local ecosystem and have a positive environmental impact at the same time!

On the other hand, though, let's be careful not to make healthy eating into another obligation or source of shame. Fresh, local greens aren't going to have a net positive effect if you have to force yourself to eat them. If that sounds like you, keep in mind that the little things count, too. For example, if you hate broccoli but love fresh strawberries, remember to take advantage of them when they're in season. Or, if you like berries but can't afford to buy them fresh, you can still get a lot of their physical and energetic benefits (not to mention delicious taste) by buying them frozen instead.

Plus, there are lots of other directions you can go with kitchen magic. Like, can you remember any recipes you loved as a kid, especially if you know they were passed down in your family? If so, those are great places to start! If not, you might want to learn more about your food heritage. Traditional food from all over the world contains a lot of wisdom about nourishment and the rhythms of living with the earth. Fundamentally, no matter what recipes you choose, food made with love and attention can have a powerful magical quality.

BASIC SMOOTHIE

(makes about four cups - one large, or up to four smaller portions)

1 ripe banana

2 C frozen berries (cherries are my favorite, sometimes mixed with something else)

1 C baby spinach (optional, but you won't taste it much if your berries are fairly sweet)

½ C milk (nondairy milk like almond is fine)

½ C plain dairy or nondairy yogurt (optional, but tasty and good for your gut bacteria)

½ C fruit juice or coconut water

Add the liquids to a blender first, followed by spinach, banana and berries in that order. Blend until smooth. Some blenders are able to handle smoothies better than others, but most will do a decent job, especially if you stop and stir and/or add a little more liquid as needed. Drink right away!

SALAD BAR

I know you know how to make a salad. But have you noticed that it can be fun? I don't tend to think of salads as very exciting, but when I actually have a fancy, perfectly customized salad in front of me it's usually a different story. Plus, you can't beat the nutrients, and if you're new to cooking the prep should be pretty simple and self-explanatory. I often chop up a bunch of ingredients ahead of time so I can mix and match and feel like I'm at a restaurant.

Possible ingredients to consider:

— lettuce and/or other greens - maybe a combination of light, crunchy romaine and something darker green

— fresh herbs and/or sprouts

— chopped cucumber, bell pepper, mushroom, onion, broccoli, cauliflower, avocado, tomato

— grated or thinly sliced carrots and/or beets

— cooked chicken, chickpeas, hard boiled egg, crumbled bacon and/or shredded cheese

— croutons, toasted chickpeas or chopped nuts for salty crunch

— dressing of choice

Then, you know, do the salad thing. You might find it surprisingly good, and you might feel surprisingly good, too.

GARLICKY GUACAMOLE

Guacamole is pretty popular for good reason. It's a quick, fresh, fancy topping you can add to a lot of other foods, or snack on with chips, carrot sticks or just a spoon (I've been known to do it). The raw garlic in this one is an immune-boosting bonus.

1 avocado

2 t lime juice

2 cloves (or 2 t) minced garlic

¼ t salt

Red pepper flakes or hot sauce to taste

1 small tomato (optional)

Peel and seed avocado, mash with other ingredients. Dice tomato and stir in if using. That's it!

GERMAN CHOCOLATE DATE BALLS

I find it hard to believe how good these are.

8 oz dried dates, pitted

¾ C unsweetened shredded coconut

¼ C toasted pecan pieces

1 t vanilla

¼ t salt

¼ C cocoa powder (or more)

Soak dates in water for a few minutes, then drain. Puree in a food processor with vanilla, cocoa powder and salt. When fairly smooth, add coconut and pecans and process until barely combined. Roll into balls, adding more cocoa if the mixture is too sticky.

If you want, you can roll the finished balls in more cocoa, nuts or coconut. Think about how weirdly much these taste like German chocolate cake.

ON DISABILITY AND CIRCUMSTANCE

Of course, here's a big difference between choosing not to do something (or, just putting off thinking about it until it kind of unchooses you) and actually being unable to do that thing due to circumstances that are outside your control. That goes for physical and mental health, but also things like literally not having the time or space to do a certain practice (I've had small children, I know how that one goes).

And of course, there are all kinds of reasons that a person might not be able to do any exercise in this book. You might not be able to make a vision board because you don't have any glue or magazines. Since there can be so much shaming around productivity and living conditions, though, I felt like this section deserved a special disclaimer.

The thing about Witchcraft is that there are always, always other ways. It's nice to have a comfortable, pleasant work environment and living space, but there have always been competent Witches who don't. When it comes to disability, specifically, it's worth considering that in many times and places, magic has been *primarily* the province of those who are less able to do more typical types of work for one reason or another.

So I guess I'm just saying, as usual, take all this with a grain of salt and figure out how to make the magic work in a way that works for you.

SPELLCASTING PART 2: RESONANT ACTION

Feeling a little more grounded? Great! Let's get back to spellwork, and how we can bring more of that earth energy into it.

You may have heard of the Law of Attraction, and if you haven't you've probably heard of *The Secret*, which was a problematic but pretty successful attempt to popularize some ancient occult wisdom. It's based on the alchemists' axiom *as above, so below*, which is sometimes called the principle of correspondence.

The first part of this is the idea that things in the natural world tend to mirror each other on a number of different levels. A popular example is the structure of the solar system, and how similar it is to the structure of an atom—there are certain patterns that seem to work in our universe, and these patterns tend to be repeated in a variety of ways. In modern language, we could describe them as *fractal*, meaning any pattern in which the structure of each part is the same as the structure of the whole—for example, a tree, where a small branch can look strikingly similar to the tree itself. This multi-level mirroring is often a matter of physical structure, but can play out in other ways, too. For example, the breath is a very magically powerful concept not only because it fuels our physical bodies, but also because it provides us with an embodied experience of the pattern of expansion and contraction that we encounter in so many other ways, from day and night to growth and decay.

The second part of the principle of correspondence is the idea that things that share these patterns (or any other characteristics) are in some way magically linked. For example, the practice of making a doll to resemble a person (popularly known as a voodoo dolls, though the dolls may have more of a history in European Witchcraft than in Vodoun) then interacting with the doll to bring help or harm to the person it represents is based on the principle of correspondence. So is the doctrine of signatures (the traditional idea that if a plant resembled a human organ, it was probably a useful remedy for treating that part of the body). This may be an outdated idea in terms of mainstream medicine, but it's still a mainstay of magical work.

So, remember how we came up with a magical intention? In order to give it greater power to manifest in the physical world, you can create a physical spell with symbolic objects that represent your goals. Doing this has a few functions: it gets your body in touch with what your mind is trying to accomplish, it speaks to your subconscious mind (which often responds better to symbolism than to literal language), and it probably makes you take what you're doing a little more seriously.

The most common example of a simple physical spell is lighting a candle to symbolize your intention. Ideally, choose a color related to what you desire, such as red for love or green for money. You can find a lot of magical charts of correspondence listing the symbolic meanings of different colors, smells, shapes, numbers, herbs, crystals, times of day and all sorts of other components, but the most important thing is that the symbolism feels meaningful to you. If you like the idea of researching symbolism, go for it! On the other hand, if you want to use a sky-blue candle because it reminds you of how good you felt on a summer day, that works, too.

When you're ready, hold your candle, taking a few minutes to relax as much as possible and bring your intention to mind. If you want, you can carve the words of your intention or a symbol that represents it onto the candle (thumbtacks work pretty well for this). Visualize your wish coming true, bringing up all of that sensory detail. Again, bring to mind the things you might see, feel, hear, smell and taste, and allow yourself to experience the emotions that would come along with them. Think about what you would say or do if your wish came true. Feel the energy in your body, and imagine some of that energy flowing into the candle, charging it with the power of your intention.

Put the candle in a secure location. If it feels right, speak your intention out loud, then light the candle and let it burn for as long as possible. Burning the whole thing is ideal, but certainly not required (and not worth risking a fire hazard). Do keep in mind that this is a pre-enchanted candle, though, if you're ever tempted to use it again in the future. Wait and see what happens!

roots.

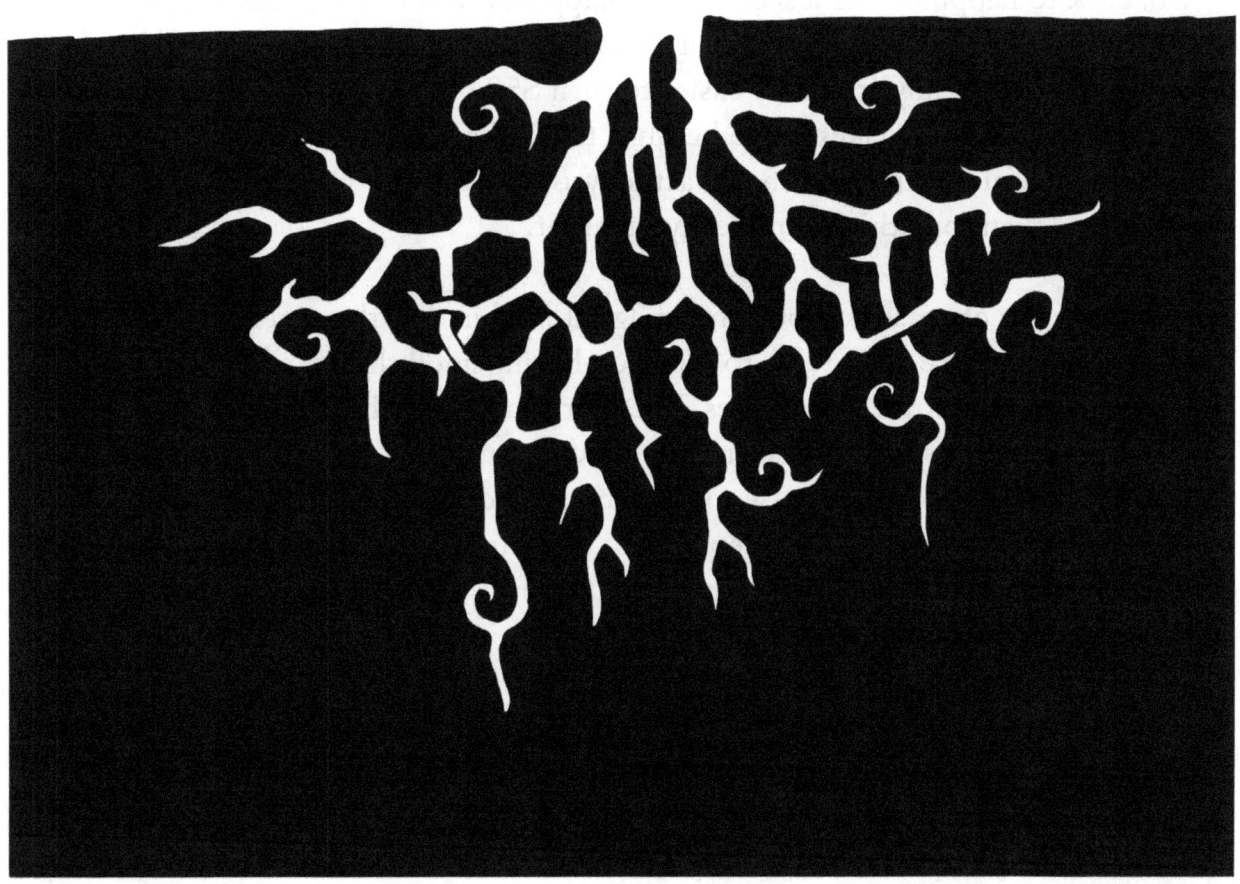

ON THE LAW OF ATTRACTION

The Secret didn't get too much further into magical theory, but it did popularize the belief that you can attract more of what you want into your life by focusing more on positive feelings about the things you desire, and less on your fears and other "negative" feelings. This created waves of mixed feelings in the magical community.

My personal take on it is that it's fundamentally correct, in the sense that clarifying and focusing on what you want is the foundation of a lot of powerful magic. Unfortunately, though, people also walked away from it with some pretty damaging ideas—in particular, the idea that if you don't have something you want it's because you're just not happy enough or you don't want it enough and, worse, that if bad things have ever happened to you it's somehow your fault. Unfortunately, these feelings of guilt and fear of what one's own subconscious might manifest are some of the most harmful "negative" feelings out there.

So, back to happiness for a second. Yes, happiness can be magically helpful. So can health, useful skills, good looks, popularity, social privilege and having a good head start on your goals. Magically, it's much easier to turn $50 into $100 than it is to make $50 from scratch, and this makes sense because that's the same way having an advantage works in material terms—and magic actually *is* the way the world works in material terms, rather than something completely different.

The way this often shakes out on a magical level is that the more good things you have already, the more you're able to focus on having good things, and the more you're able to believe into future possibilities. The more bad things have happened to you, the harder it is to expect good things, and the harder you might have to work to believe in your desires. This also makes sense, and is a big part of the way internalized oppression works. As bad as being physically deprived of the things you want or need can be, being deprived of the ability to believe in them might be even worse (and is part of the challenge of dealing with systemic trauma).

To put it another way, people tend to think that The Law of Attraction means that *people get what they deserve*, which I think is very misleading. I think the truth is more like *what people get is influenced by what they expect*, and, unfortunately, *what we expect is partly related to life experiences outside of our control*.

The good news is that magical practice also has a long and powerful history as a tool for marginalized and oppressed communities and desperate last-ditch situations. Yes, certain societal advantages can give you a leg up magically and materially, but there are also less obvious advantages, and plenty of workarounds and back doors. For one thing, it's hard to beat the powerful purity of intention that tends to go along with very basic desires like the desire to express yourself freely and find a way to thrive in the world or, for that matter, the desire to have the basic necessities of life. Fairy tales are full of penniless and powerless protagonists who find that their position is somehow secretly a magical advantage. While it's true that magic doesn't always level the playing field as absolutely as we might like it to, it's also true that you can start right now from wherever you are and there's no upper limit to your potential, regardless of your background.

ON BUILDING SPELLS

When you create your own physical spell for a particular purpose, there are two main things to keep in mind. First, while a simple candle spell can be fine, if you want to get fancier it's good to focus on making things immersive. Think about how you could bring in different types of action and sensory experience. Second, keep the symbolism in mind for as many components as possible. So, for example, burning incense while you light your candle is a good addition—it adds to the mood and helps with sensory engagement—but it's double good if you pick a type of incense that also symbolizes or reminds you of your intention.

As with the color of your candle, the most important aspect of symvolism is whether something reminds *you* of your intention. It can also be powerful to consider traditional associations, though. You can find tables of correspondence for almost any type of purpose and material (they rarely match up 100% and are *never* comprehensive—even these charts are powerfully influenced by the creator's specific tradition and individual experience), but here's a small chart to give you an idea of how they work.

Purpose	Color	Common Associations	Animal Symbolism
Protection	White, purple	Salt, mirrors, weapons, light	Wolf, hawk, dove
Prosperity	Green, gold	Money, food, and other luxuries	Dragon, rabbit, frog
Healing	Blue, green	Water, medicinal herbs, sun	Snake, bear, butterfly
Love	Pink, red	Roses, hearts, scented oil, apple	Swan, rabbit, dog
Power	Red, black	Fire, blood, anything hard to obtain	Bat, deer, horse
Wisdom	White, black	Books or writing tolls, eyes	Owl, fox, cat

There are also a few common alternatives to candle spells that you could use as starting points. These include knot spells (tie a knot in a cord while visualizing your intention, sealing it in place), charm bags (collect or create materials symbolizing your intention and store them in a bag or other container to carry with you or leave in a relevant location), tea or soup spells (stir your intention into the liquid while you work, then drink it), and burning a symbolic item to release something from your life. You can also use your imagination, of course, but that should give you an idea of how a lot of Witches get started in terms of customizing spells for specific intentions.

ON DATES, TIMES, AND PHASES OF THE MOON

The bottom line with magical timing is that there can be a lot of nuance if you want to get fancy about it. Just like you can pick out colors, smells and other symbols for your spell, you can pick appropriate times of day, days of the week, seasons and dates related to your goal.

A lot of this is based on astrological correspondence. You pick the planet that best aligns with your intention (for example, Venus for love—you can easily look up more of these associations), and then you can also look up what dates and times of day are considered especially auspicious for Venus magic.

Here's the thing about astrology, though: it's really complicated. I also have to admit that I don't know that much about it. For some people astrology is an important part of Witchcraft, but I think that's a good example of the way there are so many potential paths that we all need to find our own areas of focus and, consequently, areas we can more or less ignore most of the time.

That's not to say that I have any problem with astrology, specifically! Occasionally it seems like the whole world is going a little crazy, and when I ask a knowledgeable friend what's up with the stars, they'll often have an answer that makes lots of sense. I also think that if your knowledge of astrology is limited to what your sun sign is, it's well worth getting at least a free version of your birth chart (you can generate one online), which might give you some insight into subtle trends in your life. Maybe you'll find it so interesting that you get really into it and learn a lot more about astrology!

If you don't actually go down that path, though, let me just say that I have mixed feelings about the value of astrological timing. Only a little bit mixed, really. To be honest, looking up precise dates and times that don't have any meaning to me personally has never felt particularly valuable. When I think about magical timing, I think a lot more about things I can see and feel, like the moon cycle. I wasn't always aware of it, but once I started checking in with the moon I've definitely noticed that it affects my energy. Full moon vibes tend to be creative, a bit intense and especially good for lots of types of spellwork, while new moon's quiet can be an equally good opportunity for introspection and banishing.

Over time, I've also noticed that the season tends to have a big impact on my magical experience. I find it easiest to get magical results from around Halloween to the Winter Solstice, and to some extent from Mayday to the Summer Solstice. Many magical folks tend to notice similar trends, though interestingly we seem to vary in terms of which of the two solstice periods we experience more powerfully. Those endless days around the ends of February and August, on the other hand, are times that nobody loves, and I would probably keep it simple and avoid new magical projects unless the need is urgent.

If you want a bit more than that, days of the week are pretty easy to integrate, too. In English and a lot of other European languages, they're named for magical powers. Monday is for the moon, Tuesday for Tir, Wednesday for Odin, Thursday for Thor, Friday for Freya, Saturday for Saturn, and Sunday for the Sun. These all have their own particular associations, but since Freya is a powerful patron of magic, Friday is a good bet for general-purpose magic. Plus, of course, it's a day that a lot of us have powerful good feelings about for weekend reasons, and that sort of thing counts, too. Along similar lines, planning your ritual on your birthday or anniversary, the day you have the most free time or right before your big test is just as good as any other kind of time-based consideration, and often more important.

ON PROSPERITY MAGIC

The second category of popular spell that deserves special consideration is money magic. People tend to have a lot of feelings around this. Some people seem to think that it's wrong to cast spells for money, as though mixing spirituality with finance is some kind of taboo—and this isn't surprising, since many of us are stuck between a spiritual culture that devalues the desire to enjoy worldly existence, and a capitalist culture that makes it way too easy to obsess about money. Plus, we've seen a lot of intersections of money and spirit gone wrong, from powerful religious institutions to deeply questionable gurus. We're still born with an innate desire to appreciate good and beautiful things, though, so this gets complicated.

Even when we can agree that enjoying things is great, money is an extra weird thing to enjoy. Isn't its value based on scarcity? Is it wrong to wish for more money, knowing that so many others are suffering without it? These are real questions and there are no simple answers. Sometimes people say you should focus more on the thing you want to buy, like a vacation, and less on how you're going to get it. If what you really want is a vacation, I think that's a great strategy! Sometimes, though, you just want money, and these complications don't stop most of us from wanting it. If anything, they just make us weird about admitting it.

If you think you might want money but have mixed feelings about it, the first thing to do is try to get as much clarity around that as you can—maybe do some journaling. Write about whether you really, really want that money. It's actually possible that you don't care that much, but you just sort of assume that you do—and if that's you, you might do better to focus on the *I want a vacation/new shoes/to get my bills paid off* approach. If you really do want money, how much do you want and why? Ask yourself whether you really think that getting that money would cause anyone harm, or if it might even bring some good into the world. Write anything that scares you about that money, or holds you back. Basically, just try to get all those complicated feelings out there on the page.

It's very common to feel like you might not deserve more money, which is reasonable because of all the people who don't have enough. Really, though, money doesn't seem to have a lot to do with what anybody deserves. Think about all the people who deserve money but don't have it, and the people who do have it but probably don't deserve it.

Resolve, whether you get that money or not, to do your best to bring joy and prosperity to others around you in your own way.

Besides these basic issues, give a bit of thought to how you might like the money to arrive. As I mentioned before, I'm not a big believer in the idea that you must create a structure for the money to get to you—like applying for a bunch of jobs—because in my experience the path it takes is sometimes quite surprising. I will say, though, that fear of the path it will take could definitely hinder your efforts. For example, if you're a freelancer and you subconsciously associate more money with more difficult clients, that could cause complications (I have some personal experience with this one). You might really want the money, but dislike the hassle of dealing with clients, so that's a conflict of interests that could end up holding you back. For this reason, I think it's worth considering what path you would *prefer* for the money to take and, once you figure that out, it might make sense to take steps to smooth that path a bit—such as filling out those job applications.

As far as actual spellcrafting for prosperity, I guess I do have a few tips. Start with a dollar amount that seems plausible, and if that works out you can always go for more if you still want it. Practice being as generous as you reasonably can in both monetary and non-monetary ways, and accepting various kinds of generosity from others—this should help you to build or rebuild a mental model of the universe as a more generous, financially supportive place. I also like to keep a piggy bank around, which I think of as kind of a friendly spirit-guardian of my finances. I put in whatever kind of money I feel like I can spare (starting with small change only, but increasing over time). When it's full, I use the money for something fun and luxurious that makes me feel more prosperous.

These are little tricks that work for me, but fundamentally I feel like about 90% of financial magic is getting super clear on your intention. If that's hard for you, don't feel bad. It's not your fault that money is complicated and you probably have an uncomfortable relationship with it—that's capitalism. But, if you still want to work on money magic, work on those attitudes. On the material end, a simple candle or similar spell should work just fine.

Opposite is a coloring page that you can use as part of a prosperity spell if you want. You can also download a printable version at http://lauragyre.com/creativerituals. Focus on your specific financial intention while coloring the image, then use it however you like to complete your spell.

ON ALTARS

One particular thing you might want to set up to make your space more magical, especially if you like working with physical spells, is an altar. This doesn't have to be anything fancy. It can start with a mantle, shelf or small table. The basic idea is to place objects representing your practice there. Like the candle spell, this kind of practice helps to bring the mental work you're doing into the physical realm.

A really common thing to do with an altar is to physically represent the elements. The traditional occult tools for the elements are a knife (sometimes called an athame, representing a sharp mind and the power to make decisions) for air, a pentacle (something round and decorated with a five-pointed star inside a circle, representing material wealth and physical wellbeing) for earth, a cup (representing love and intuition) for water, and a wand for fire and will. There are also a lot of variations you can get into while still maintaining an elemental theme—for example, a feather or bell for air, a rock, crystal, dish of salt or something made of clay for earth, a shell or container of actual water for water, and a candle or something made of metal for fire are also popular choices. Of course, you can also add non-elemental objects that have magical significance for you, like things collected from your favorite nature spot, gifted by loved ones or saved from special rituals you took part in.

Once you have an altar going it should remind you of your commitment to magical practice and maintaining a magical space in your home, but there are also some practical things you can do with it. Depending on location, you might want to sit in front of it for meditation practice. You can also use it as a place to burn spell candles or do other magical work, and maybe store small magical items like tarot cards when they're not in use.

Another good thing to do is to make offerings at your altar. I like to use an elemental theme for offerings, too, so every day I try to set out a bite of food and a little water, light a small candle and burn incense or herbs. (If you make offerings like this, try to eat any leftover food before it goes bad, or return it directly to the earth rather than throwing any offerings in the trash).

Again, you can offer whatever feels right to you. Dedicate the offerings to God, Goddess, the gods, your helping spirits, the universe or your own highest self—pretty much whatever resonates with you and feels comfortable. You can also start to think about working with specific gods and spirits if you feel drawn to that sort of thing.

ON GODS, GODDESSES AND SPIRITS

As mentioned somewhat already, there are a wide variety of views on Witchcraft as a religion. If you're not drawn to regard it as a religious practice or to work with gods, goddesses or other spirits, that's fine. It can still be useful to build an altar and make offerings, but you might want to think of them as offerings to the universe at large or the best, most perfect version of yourself. It can be quite useful to find something outside your everyday ego that you can feel somewhat reverent toward and look to for intuitive guidance at times.

On the other hand, many Witches work a lot with spirits, from a total dedication to a particular God or Goddess to an animist perspective in which everything has a spirit you can learn to relate to. Besides deities, the spirits that Witches might work with can include plant, animal and other nature spirits, spirits of particular places, angels, daemons, fairies and departed ancestors. Spirits can also be unique and difficult to place into these categories. Some Witches (in chaos magic style) even choose to work with fictional characters or "spirits" they invent themselves.

There are a lot of different ways to relate to these beings, as well as these ideas. A chaos magic perspective is that there's no particular reality behind any of the descriptions, but going through the motions of working with a spirit can be a tool for getting into an important type of mindstate for spiritual work. Personally, I feel like that perspective itself is a useful tool, but not the whole story. Plus, there's a kind of tongue-in-cheek attitude where you can go around saying one thing at your altar and another as you explain what you're doing to your others that strikes me as somewhat lacking in integrity and not entirely respectful to any deities you didn't make up after watching TV.

More classical perspectives vary from hard polytheism (in which different deities are regarded as having entirely discrete, independent existence) to soft polytheism (which works more with a general sense of divinity that can be addressed in different archetypal forms depending on your personality and needs in a specific moment).

To be honest, I often find this entire discussion somewhat beside the point. A lot of traditional religions have some things to say about gods, but they all pretty much agree that humans don't really understand them, and I think that's a pretty good place to start. If you feel drawn to work with particular gods or spirits (maybe don't start with anybody who has a reputation for being especially scary or dangerous) start by dedicating some offerings and prayers to them. Learn more about them and how they were traditionally worshipped, but also trust your intuition and try different things. It is generally a good idea to build up a practice slowly, developing an ongoing relationship.

This might also be a good time to check back in with that playful, creative perspective. You don't have to write a thesis on your beliefs before you start to make offerings and prayers. If you're curious about the concept but not drawn in a particular direction, we'll talk more about searching for guidance in the next section. In the meantime, general altar work is a good foundation for devotional practice and a good place to start in terms of this overall practice.

A NOTE ON CULTURAL APPROPRIATION (PART 1)

This note is mainly for white people, like myself, who would like to practice Witchcraft in a way that's respectful to non-European cultural traditions. Although there are unfortunately exceptions, most of us would really like to do this. Our interest in traditions from other cultures is generally deep, driven by a sincere desire to appreciate wisdom and spirit in their many forms, and we definitely don't want to hurt anybody. Many of us even come to Witchcraft out of a desire to find spiritual roots in our own cultures, rather than participating in appropriative borrowing. Unfortunately, there are some trends in Witchcraft and related pagan religions that contribute to ongoing (if generally unintentional) harm.

This has a lot to do with context. The fact is, European colonizers have done a lot of harm to other people's cultures over the centuries, disrespecting them, disrupting them and in some cases wiping them out entirely. This historical damage certainly isn't the fault of contemporary white people who weren't even around at the time when it was most actively taking place, but if we want to think of ourselves as part of the solution rather than part of the problem, we need to do what we can to reduce the ongoing effects of the damage and certainly not to perpetuate it.

To generalize pretty broadly, the most common type of harm related to Witchcraft comes when we're attracted to some spiritual practice or object and want to adopt it without proper understanding and relationship to its cultural context. This can lead to incorrect practices that are disrespectful to any entities involved, and also the spreading of misinformation and ongoing erasure of any modern people who are practicing their traditional beliefs in a way that's often less visible than whatever white converts are doing.

So, for example, what if you feel called to work with a certain non-European god or goddess? While some traditions are quite reasonably closed to outsiders, others are more than willing to teach sincere, respectful aspirants. Your best bet is probably to seek out a (local, if possible) group of traditional practitioners who are willing to share their beliefs and teach you about appropriate and inappropriate approaches. Also, keep in mind that many worship practices take place in the context of a community. If you really want to work with a particular god but you don't want anything to do with his followers, that's a big red flag and you might want to spend some time figuring out what's going on with that. Of course, once you know more you can decide whether you're willing to commit to what that path actually entails, and how well it might mesh with your other practices.

Similar principles apply to sacred objects. Some are generally considered appropriate for anyone to use, but if you want to use them it's a good idea to do your research and make sure you know how to use and care for them respectfully. It's also worth considering who profits from your purchases. If I ever want to use spiritual items from other cultures, I do my best to buy them from traditional makers.

If all that seems a bit convoluted, think about the changes that have come along with the popularization of yoga. Almost everyone knows that yoga is Indian, and some prominent Indian teachers have actively worked to spread it to a wider audience. Pretty much everyone believes that it's ok for white people to do yoga, but since it's become popular with Americans, the commonly understood meaning of yoga has started to change. While most Indians still associate it with religious practice, many Americans (even Americans who love yoga) now regard it mainly as a fitness activity. Plus, mainstream yoga has become increasingly commercial and celebrity-driven. Most of the best-known celebrities are white Americans, and much of the money for luxury yoga goods also tends to go to white people.

No individual person can stop this kind of trend, but we can all do our best to be aware of it and continue to center the teachings (and financial support) of the cultures that have generously shared their wisdom with us. Of course, the short answer to the question of what to do about this is that you *can* do whatever you want, and nobody is going to kick you out of Witch Club. But wouldn't it be better if we could do more to support other polytheist and animist traditions, which could be our natural allies?

When it comes to specific European pantheons and traditions, it might be worth looking into your own family roots to see whether there are ancestral practices that particularly appeal to you. On the other hand, picking, choosing and following your heart when it comes to adopting these practices isn't usually such a big deal, politically. This is because there's no real danger of European people getting pushed out of their own traditions by others, or becoming invisible in those traditions. Of course, whether mixing pantheons is a good idea on a magical and spiritual level is an entirely different question, but it seems to work for some people. If you're not sure about it, that's a question you can take up directly with any gods or spirits you'd like to start working with.

MORE EXPERIMENTS WITH EARTH

1. Touch the earth! Spending time in nature is good, but in this case I mean the actual dirt. Walk around outside with bare feet if you can. This is a great way to feel the energy of the earth, and may even help reduce inflammation and regulate biorhythms. And did you know that there are antidepressant bacteria (mycobacterium vaccae) in soil?

Gardening is a good hobby if you could use more earth in your life. If doing it outdoors is impractical, even a small indoor garden can provide some contact with soil, the energy of living things and maybe some delicious fresh herbs.

2. Once you've spent some time working with earth, you might want to make some art about it. Starting a nature sketchbook is one great way of paying more attention to the world around you. Or, you could try working with clay for the most literal kind of earth art experience. If you haven't done a lot of it, sculpting can be really fun to play around with, providing a more tactile experience than most kinds of art. Dancing is another creative activity with a strong embodiment component, and drumming adds a rhythmic element that echoes the natural rhythms of the body and the earth.

3. Make your own candles for spellwork and offerings. I usually make a batch of my own at least once a year, around Imbolc. This is a good opportunity to use natural, high-quality materials and weave more of your own energy into your ritual tools. Plus, it's fun and makes your house smell great!

To use this method you will need cotton twine, an empty glass jar you don't mind parting with and at least a pound of beeswax. Put some beeswax chunks or pellets in the jar (chunks take a long, long time to melt, so you can try grating them if you want). Put an inch or so of water in a pan and set the jar of wax in it, then start to heat on low.

These details are important for a few reasons. For one, wax is really hard to get out of stuff, so if you put it directly in your pan the pan will never be the same. Also, if the wax gets too hot it could catch on fire, and keeping it in a larger pan of water helps to control the temperature (similar to a double boiler). Plus, we want to create a fairly deep pool of melted wax, which is easier in a tall, narrow container like a jar. BUT! It's important to put the jar in the heating pan right away, because suddenly exposing a cold jar to boiling water can shatter it.

The melting step will take a while. Add more wax as you go, until the jar is fairly full. While you wait, you can set up a space to hang your drying candles. Place two chairs back to back a couple of feet apart, and balance some kind of stick or pole (maybe more than one) between their backs. Lay out newspaper under the poles to protect your floor from dripping wax.

Cut lengths of twine about twelve to eighteen inches long (your candles will be less than half this height). Hold each piece by one end and carefully dip in the liquid wax to cover as much of the string as possible (it's ok to skip the end you're holding). Hang the string up over one of the poles, and repeat with the rest of your pieces.

After all the strings have been coated and you have a jar full of liquid wax, pick up a wick (wax-coated string, which should now feel a bit stiff) by the center and dip both ends as deep into the jar as you can. If managing two ends at once is tricky, you can hold the ends apart and dip one at a time. Either way, do this step fairly quickly—if you leave the wick in the wax for more than a moment, the previous layers will melt back off every time and fail to accumulate. Then, hang it back up and repeat with all the other wicks.

That's actually pretty much all there is to it. You just repeat that dipping process a whole lot of times, until the candles are as thick as you want. If the wax level starts to get low, you can refill the jar as much as you want.

These candles tend to be lumpier than the commercial kind, at least when I make them. When you're done, you can try rolling them on a flat surface while still warm if you'd like to smooth them out a bit. You can also roll warm candles in herbs, flower petals or other materials for magical or aesthetic purposes if you want to get a bit fancier.

4. Eat mindfully. Regardless of what you eat and where it comes from, mealtime is a great time to remember the special relationship between food and life energy. Start by thinking about how to make your meal appealing, even if you're eating alone. Do you like the food? Are you using the dishes you like? What will you be seeing and hearing while you eat? If you often eat while watching TV or browsing the internet, consider a more mindful focus for at least some of your meals, for example eating outside if the weather is nice. You could also say a quick prayer of thanks, take a moment of silence to consider the source of the food, light a candle on the table or gather some energy to direct into the food before you start to eat.

5. Tone your vagus nerve. This nerve, which passes from the brain through most of the major organs, is an important part of the parasympathetic nervous system that helps to downregulate stress and contributes to the proper function of body systems from digestion to circulation to hormonal balance. Its function is also improved by a variety of traditional spiritual practices, including chanting, deep breathing, mindful movement, meditation, and fasting—plus laughing, and getting massage. Pick your favorites and help your nervous system get in shape.

6. On a more whimsical note, another way to bring more magic into your space is to make a fairy house. This is an exercise in creativity and an offering to local spirits that you can do in your own way. Many examples (which you can find online) start with natural materials, some fancy decorative elements like ribbons and marbles and often a hot glue gun. Design one for a natural environment (maybe near the base of a tree), your porch or an indoor planter. If you have any kids around, consult them for further ideas.

7. Practice gratitude. Loosely based on the principle that things tend to influence similar things, there's a common belief that it's easy to attract more of whatever you're feeling. So, there's a lot of weird advice floating around about how to "stay positive," if you want to attract more happy feelings. Much of this advice can be pretty useless if not downright damaging, since emotions you suppress just stay in your subconscious mind and continue to mess stuff up while you insist you're not feeling them.

The thing I love about gratitude practice is that it's a way to increase the positive energy in your life without having to deny anything else. No matter what's going on, there are probably things in your life you can appreciate, especially if you take the time to look for them. Plus, I've found this practice pretty effective at creating a cycle of positivity. Like it or not, when you feel good you're more likely to notice more good things around you—and moods can be contagious. The more genuinely good feeling you can muster, the more you'll tend to receive from those around you, too.

For example, when I started to experiment with gratitude I decided to try a month-long daily practice without telling anyone. I felt good and noticed a lot of positive things happening in my life, but the most dramatic thing happened after the month was over. Three days in a row, my partner asked me out of the blue if I was feeling ok. I was feeling fine—I just wasn't actively practicing gratitude anymore, and apparently it showed.

The tricky thing is that gratitude works best if you can really feel it in your body, and that sometimes takes a little work to discover. My favorite practice is to make a section in my magical journal and write a list of things I'm grateful for every day. I try to make the items specific, include sensory detail in my descriptions to conjure more sensation, and avoid falling back on the same rote list too often. This can be simple and fun, but if you find it tedious that sort of defeats the purpose, so you might need to explore different options or at least switch it up from time to time.

Other possibilities include making art about things you're grateful for, thanking people and starting conversations about gratitude, or picking a time of day to visualize real or imagined scenes that fill you with love and other pleasant feelings.

8. Gather at your hearth. You can certainly do all these practices on your own, but home practices also tend to relate to family and hospitality. Pretty much all this work can be done in a group as well, and most earth practices are particularly well suited for sharing. For example, you could get together with friends for a home-cooked meal or a potluck, a candle-making party, a picnic in the woods, a session of energy experimentation or an evening of drumming and dancing. With a group of like-minded friends, you could even explore the idea of regular monthly or seasonal gatherings for assorted creative and/or magical purposes.

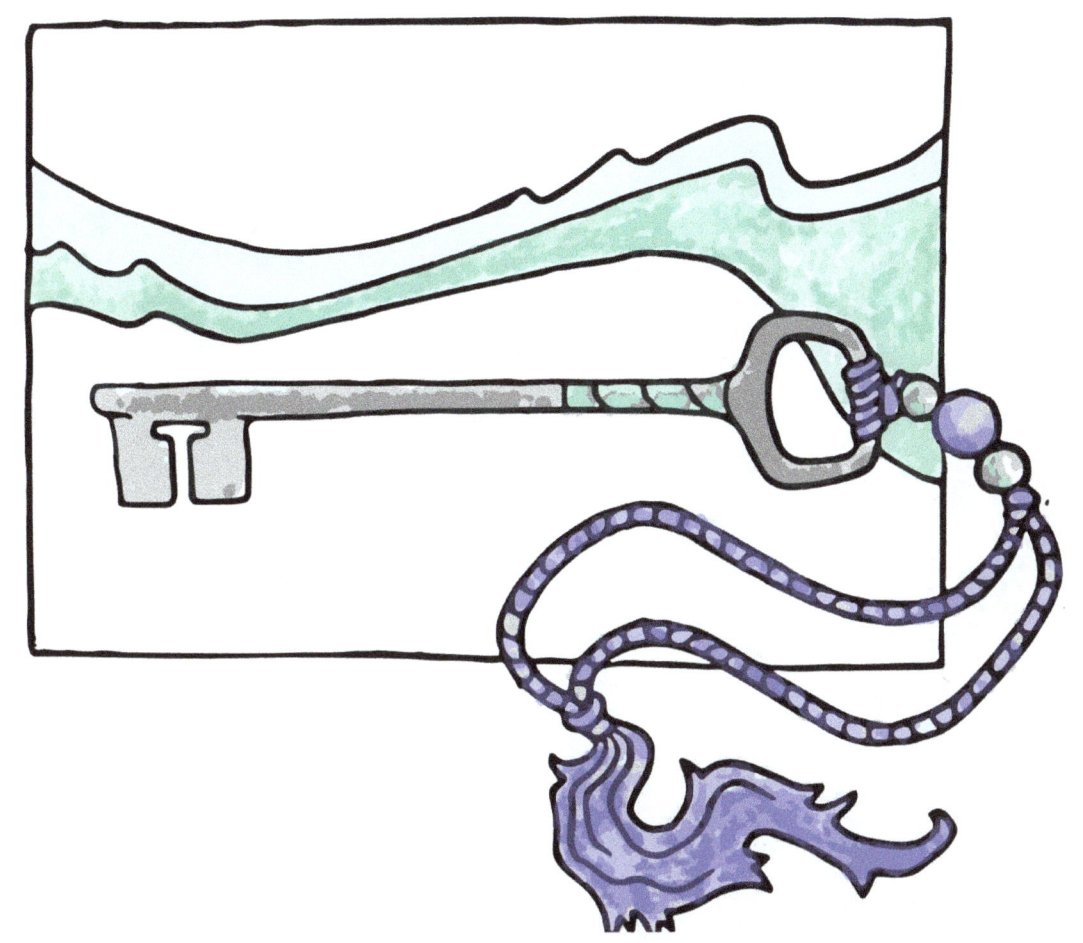

III. GOING WITH THE FLOW

So far, we've been touching on the aspects of magic that are closest to the material and scientific. Is it magical, does it create *change in accordance with will*, to sort out your desires, build a to-do list and accomplish your goals? You could certainly say that it does. The Earth-based stuff feels a bit more, well, touchy-feely, but we even have some scientific theories about the way that energy passes between our bodies. That doesn't take away from the magic, but it can all feel a bit concrete.

Water is where it gets kind of weird, not to mention a bit harder to put words around. Water is the realm of the subconscious mind, of dreams and trance states and creative intuition. These aspects of human experience are incredibly important to magical and spiritual practice. At least, they're just as important as the conscious mind, and much more likely to be overlooked. Have you ever had the feeling that you wanted something very badly, but just couldn't make yourself take any of the steps to move toward it? Very often, this kind of experience is due to misalignment of the conscious and subconscious minds. If you're not sure what's going on in your subconscious, it's very easy to hide from things you really want subconsciously, while sabotaging your own attempts to get whatever your conscious mind thinks you *should* want instead.

The subconscious is also largely the realm of the nonverbal mind. As with the body, symbolism is the best form of communication here. In fact, the subconscious mind sometimes communicates *through* the body, by way of that gut intuition or some kind of nagging physical symptom. While logical thinking allows us to identify and work to solve problems as well as clearly communicate precise ideas to others, intuitive thinking—which often occurs in imagery before we're able to put it into words—helps us make connections between ideas that seem to be unrelated, and process vast amounts of sensory data much faster and more sensitively than our rational minds are able to.

Ideally, we would have easy access to both of these processes, moving effortlessly between them in response to circumstance. Unfortunately, our intuitive and visual modes of processing are rarely encouraged—or at least are valued less than logical thought—and are sometimes outright shamed. Plus, we're sometimes unable to disengage our hyper-rational patterns and relax into a creative mindstate due to unresolved trauma. The bottom line is, for one reason or another, many of us are dangerously deficient in water magic and could use a lot more of it in our lives.

There's also a kind of elemental balance backlash that sometimes happens when someone has a powerfully watery nature. If that person is lucky, they may be able to stay strong in their creative ability and intuition, but they might pick up the message that it's impossible to be intuitive *and* logical at the same time. Whether we're in tune with our intuition or not, almost all of us could stand to integrate these two ways of knowing more fully, because they work much better together.

ON CHECKING IN WITH YOUR SUBCONSCIOUS

If you only have a minute, using the gut check from the earth section is a good way to tune in to your intuitive guidance before making a decision. If you'd like a little more information, though, this is a great way to use creative imagery to get it. Think of a situation that's confusing you. For example, I learned this method from the book *Wild Money* by Luna Jaffe, who suggests using it to learn more about your financial situation (but you can apply the same process to any other subject, too). Draw a picture of the thing you'd like to know more about—in this case, your relationship with money. Make it quick and simple, don't allow yourself to overthink it, and certainly don't worry about your artistic ability.

Before you move on, look at your picture and title it. This is an important step, so don't be tempted to skip it! For example, the first time I tried this exercise I drew myself with one hand inside a spiral and titled it, "I don't know what's in there," which was a pretty accurate assessment of my financial situation at the time. Once you get your title, you can also examine the details more closely. *Why did you choose the colors you used? How is any character who shows up in the drawing feeling? And so on.* It's a simple process, but a great way to become more aware of some of the things that are occupying your subconscious mind.

This may not be fine art, but it's a pretty good representation of how I sometimes feel about my finances.

ON THE POWER OF IMAGERY

This is just one example of the way the subconscious mind tends to communicate well through symbolic imagery. In some ways, the pairing of conscious and subconscious mind is analogous to verbal and visual information processing. Of course, there are lots of types of nonverbal information, from instrumental music to scent to physical sensation, but even though we're kind of out of practice, most humans are still pretty good at picking up a lot of information visually. You know that saying that a picture is worth a thousand words? It's true, or at least it's fairly easy to write a thousand words describing the nuance of a single image. This level of detail is one that we don't typically notice when casually looking at things, but on an intuitive level we may absorb it automatically.

When we have a gut feeling about something, it's often because our brains have sorted through millions of visual and other sensory details much faster and more effectively than we would have been able to put those details into words. For example, there are over forty facial muscles involved in emotional expression, but we don't have to name and count those muscle movements in order to guess what someone might be feeling.

We're sometimes disinclined to trust this kind of non-verbal information, telling ourselves that we could be misreading the situation. That's true, and our own biases do feed into what we think we see. It's at least equally true, though, that our rational assessment of a situation can be simplistic, biased, missing emotional information and downright wrong, too.

There has always been a lot of imagery and symbolism involved in spiritual and magical practice. This might be because there's a lot of nuanced information to convey, or it might just be a holdover from a time when reading was less common and visual imagery was the most efficient way of spreading information at all. It's worth noting, though, that this emphasis on imagery contributes directly to a liminal state of mind where we're able to think in a more spiritual way (a way that combines literal and symbolic thinking). In this case, the medium is definitely part of the message.

Coming from a liberal Christian home, I grew up with the idea that spiritual truth is often metaphorical. It took a long time and a lot of creative practice, though, before I was able to understand what a metaphor really is. As a kid, I guess I thought it was kind of like a code (the author of a book wants to talk about hope, maybe, but that doesn't make a very interesting story, so every time they want to say hope, they put in a butterfly instead). Then, as many high-school English teachers could tell you, you have to figure out what the symbolism means in order to decode the real story. I guess this is how I tried for a while to think about miraculous stories. Like, if we say that Jesus performed miracles, are we really just saying that he was divine and therefore worthy of emulation?

The cool thing about real symbolism, though, is that that sort of canned interpretation can't capture it at all. In 1963, high school student Bruce McAllister got so sick of having to decode the symbolism in works of literature that he decided to send surveys on symbolism to 150 popular authors to see what they had to say about the subject. About half of the authors wrote back, and the results—which apparently no one had bothered to research before—were in. Overwhelmingly, the writers denied consciously adding symbols to their work. The symbols were there, of course, and the authors were generally aware of them—but they explained that this aspect of the work had emerged *subconsciously*. As novelist Iris Murdoch wrote in response, "there is much more symbolism in ordinary life than some critics seem to realize."

This puts the idea of spiritual symbolism in an entirely different light. In a way, we could think of it as a technique that our intuitive minds use to communicate with each other, entirely (or at least mostly) bypassing our conscious minds. The symbolism that we encounter as part of magical practice—whether an actual image, or a nuanced story—may pass along deep wisdom, helping us to transform in ways we're not fully ready to consciously understand. These types of symbols are also useful for conveying information that is not only unknown to our rational minds, but sometimes so multidimensional that it doesn't fit neatly into words at all.

Of course, that's not to say that we're at the mercy of existing symbolism. We're entirely able to work with it, shape it and make it our own—but we must trust our intuition enough to let it do its thing semi-independently. This working directly with living symbols is, fundamentally, what a lot of magical practice is about, and it requires a soft, slightly arrational perspective.

For example, what were the alchemists really up to with their elemental work? They were certainly working with actual metals, trying very hard to turn lead into gold. Later thinkers often described this as a symbolic process, suggesting that their real goal was to refine a spiritual practice with the goal of becoming immortal, somehow cloaking it all in respectable pseudo-science. And yes, there's plenty of evidence that immortality was on their minds, but this is because they actually were doing both. To an alchemist, the symbolism was really in the metals, and so working with the metals was a way of becoming spiritually refined, too.

Building this sort of practice in your own life is largely a matter of developing a more conscious relationship with your intuitive mind and gradually accumulating trust that whatever it's working on is valid, important, and probably worth bringing more actively into your everyday activities.

ON GETTING STARTED WITH TAROT

First of all, I want to say that tarot is another one of those complicated things. It sometimes seems like everybody is into it, but it took me years after I got into Witchcraft to get around to tackling the very involved imagery. It's a really rich system, though, if you have the time and inclination to dive into it. For one thing, the cards have elemental symbolism, with four suits representing earth, air, fire and water, which can be pretty helpful for learning about and working with this kind of magic.

If you want to experiment, try to start with a deck that you really like. If you can't find a great one, it's also fine to just go ahead and start; you could always switch to a different deck later. The Rider-Waite-Smith (also called the Rider-Waite, but illustrator Pamela Coleman Smith has been getting more credit in recent years) is classic and hard to go wrong with, since all the tarot symbolism you'll read about is clearly depicted there. If you have strong feelings about graphic style or diversity of representation, though, you might find that you connect better with a different deck.

Once you pick one out, it's a good idea to spend time looking through it and just keeping it nearby. You can also start doing readings right away. The simplest way to start is with a one card draw. Ask for advice on a particular topic, shuffle and then just pick any card. If you don't know the traditional meanings, it's worth investigating what your intuition will come up with. What detail do you notice first when you look at the card? How do you feel? Does it remind you of anyone or anything in your life? If there's a character and you had to give it a caption, what would you imagine it saying to you? This is the wonderful thing about imagery-based divination. Like any image, the cards contain much more nuanced information and range of possibility than even a few pages of text can convey, so make sure to give this visual step some space before skipping to traditional interpretation.

Once you've given it a little thought yourself, though, you might as well look your card up. If you do this often enough, you'll learn the traditional meanings of the cards as you go. Most decks come with at least a pamphlet for interpretation, and I would suggest using this at first (rather than a general tarot book) because the meanings will be specific to the imagery of your deck. It's also worth making notes about what you experience. The margins of my favorite tarot book are full of character archetypes I associate with each card and summaries of situations in which I've seen them come up. You might want to try a practice of drawing a card of the day every morning, then checking back in in the evening to see what you think it had to tell you. Over time, this kind of personal experience will add layers of nuance to your reading style, building up an understanding of symbolic meaning that goes far beyond what's easily contained in a book.

You can also start to experiment with more complicated spreads. These are ways of laying out the cards so that each position has a specific meaning—for example, one card each for the past, present and future of a situation. As you develop more formal technique, though, don't forget to keep checking in with your visual intuition. For example, in this kind of past-present-future spread, you can lay the cards out left to right and try to read them like a story. Moving from one image to the next, what's the action here? What's similar about the cards? What's changing?

I'm not going to get into a lot more detail, but I do want to add a note on reversals (reading cards that show up upside down). First of all, it's totally fine not to use them. Not everyone does, which makes the symbolism a bit less complicated (and all the cards can have positive and negative implications anyway, so it's not strictly necessary). I usually do use them, though, and the method that works best for me is to think of a reversed card as a sort of energy that's blocked.

For example, the *four of pentacles* can refer to planning. If you ask for advice and draw that card, it might be telling you to plan carefully right now. If it comes up reversed, planning might still be a good idea, but I'd also read the implication that you might feel a bit blocked or encounter challenges with your planning process. In that case, it's worth considering what could help you to plan more successfully (you can ask for advice and draw another card on that, if you want). Even the cards that have more negative or uncomfortable associations, like *death*, can be read in this way, because they all have positive aspects, too. So, *death* can be the power of major transformation, but if it comes up reversed you might be having trouble facing that kind of transformation (maybe out of fear). For me, this use of reversals is a way of valuing the constructive messages of all the cards, while recognizing that some situations feel more difficult or complex than others.

ON SCRYING

Scrying is another, simpler type of image-based divination that's easy to get started with and doesn't require any special materials. You do need something to stare at, preferably something with a cloudy or subtly changeable texture. For example, you could try gazing at actual clouds, a candle flame, smoke, a smokey crystal or a bowl of water (putting the water in a dark or reflective bowl or adding a few drops of ink or blood gives you a bit more to look at, in this case). Mirrors are historically popular and you could certainly try, but most bathroom mirrors lack the fogginess and distortion that traditional mirrors tended to have. If you really like the idea of a reflective surface, you can also get a black mirror intended for scrying.

Sit comfortably, take a few deep breaths, relax your body and drop into a light meditative state, then look at your object and let your eyes unfocus somewhat. See what you notice. This is pretty much like looking for pictures in the clouds, except that you can treat them like dream images and let your mind wander to what stories might be unfolding in the images you see, or how they might relate to whatever topic is one your mind. There can certainly be a bit of free-association involved, too—if you pick clouds or fire you may actually see a series of images unfolding, but if you try scrying with a crystal, for example, what you're actually seeing with your eyes isn't going to change much. Hopefully, the visual details will give your intuitive mind some kind of reference point as you let your imagination wander.

ON THE ART PROCESS

There are as many ways to approach art as an intuitive practice as there are artists. I'm not actually sure it's possible to create much of anything without engaging your intuition, which might be why art tends to be so magical. Even the types of project that we think of as less serious or creative, like using a coloring book or copying someone else's style, are deeply engaging to your own body and mind. Whatever you're working on, it's something you chose to do for your own reasons. You picked out the materials and colors. You bring your own history, environment and intuitive contribution to the process, whether you mean to or not.

I guess I tend to think that all art is intuitive, magical art, but if you'd like to be more aware of how your intuition functions, bring more uniqueness into your creations and come up with an endless number of new ideas, process painting can be a really helpful and interesting practice. Anyone can do it, so it's also a really great entry point for people who think of themselves as not very artistic.

If you want to try it, get some big paper and paint in a variety of colors. Nothing has to be fancy. You might actually want to choose something on the cheaper end so you'll feel more free to use it up and make mistakes, but it should also be a material you enjoy the experience of using. I sometimes just use chunky kids' markers for process drawing (especially in situations where time is limited or I'm not sure if people want to get messy) but if you have the time, space and materials you'll probably find that painting engages your senses more deeply. See if there's a way to hang your paper on the wall or lay it down on the floor—some kind of situation that will involve more full-body movement than small paper on a table—and do your best to protect your clothes and work surface so you don't have to think about those things too much while you paint.

The main thing that makes process painting special is what happens next. Instead of thinking of what you want to paint or how you want your painting to end up looking, think about *how* you want to paint right now. Think about what color or material is the most exciting and use that one first. Check in with your body and feel how it wants to move. Sweeping strokes? Tiny, repetitive motions? The painting doesn't have to stay abstract. Maybe you'll want to put some blue all over the paper, and then notice that it might be a sky. It's ok to get inspired to add particular subjects or details, but keep checking in with your immediate experience of the process.

You can paint whatever you want, but try not to get too attached to what it's becoming. If you spend an hour painting your peaceful sky scene and then suddenly notice the neon pink paint, go for it! Even if you've started to work on imagery, don't try to force it to make sense. Just notice what type of color, movement and imagery are attracting you in each moment, and let yourself bring it into your painting. You may notice once you start to work that it all makes sense in a way you didn't consciously anticipate.

The reason this is called process painting is that the focus is more on experiencing the process of creation than on what you (or certainly anybody else) will think of the painting when it's done. I think it's a really interesting tool, but as a person who does a lot of visual art with more of a specific outcome in mind, it can also get frustrating when things don't turn out the way I want. When that happens, I try to focus on those feelings. It's ok to feel mixed and powerful emotions while you work! It's also ok to end up with a painting that you're not exactly proud of, as long as the journey was interesting.

I like to remember in those difficult moments that both types of process are valuable—the unrestrained creativity of process painting, and the skillful craft of creating more precise results. At times, I do use imagery that occurred to me during process painting to create more "finished" pieces, but I try to save that for later. In order to get the most out of both ways of working, it's important to make sure the process work has plenty of space to resolve, too—not necessarily in terms of a finished product, but in terms of allowing the experience itself enough time and space to play out fully, rather than giving in to frustration and rushing back to something more familiar.

Once you get started, there are any number of variations to explore. Of course, you can use different media; clay has an interesting physicality, for example. You can also experiment with listening to different types of music while you work. Painting in a group is another possible direction (you can create individual pieces in the same space, take turns working on a few different projects or make one big painting together).

It's a good idea, in groups, to lay down some ground rules about not commenting on what you like or dislike in other people's work. Positive comments might seem innocuous, but they can still make it harder to focus on the process, rather than a premeditated outcome. Talking about how everybody is feeling as they work, on the other hand, or what comes to mind when looking at all the art can lead to some interesting conversations.

Magically speaking, this is all just good practice that helps to encourage elemental balance and increase intuitive perception, but you can also apply a similar process more directly as a form of divination or even a sort of spell. If you have a question, dream image or other mysterious idea on your mind, you can kick it around gently while you work. Images or feelings may emerge that have something to say about your theme. You could also experiment with setting a magical intention before you start to work. Just as you bring your intention into being by lighting a candle, you can also start to manifest it by creating a symbolic piece of art.

Process painting works well for this, but so does "regular" drawing or painting. When working on spells with other people, drawing might actually be my favorite method. As you imagine the outcome you desire (like a new home, which is pretty fun to draw), each person can add details to the drawing, explaining what they represent. Using process painting in this way could be a little less predictable, but possibly all the more magical as you work through an exploratory process right there on the page.

ON PROCESS WORK

This process is inspired by Arnold and Amy Mindell, psychologists who have done some really interesting work on the transformative power of choosing any image or sensation and following it closely to see where it leads. I've had great luck with this kind of thing when I want to start a project but feel like I don't have any ideas. The results tend to get surprisingly deep and magical eventually.

1. Sit or stand quietly, waiting to feel an impulse to move some part of your body even a tiny bit.

2. Start moving in that way, repeating the movement and allowing it to expand and change if it wants to.

3. As you move, notice any images that flash through your mind. Allow those images to expand and change, too.

4. Start to move as though you were one of the images that you see.

5. Do anything else (for example, making sounds, or interacting with objects) that you feel inspired to do, unfolding from that point.

6. Sketch something you just saw, felt or experienced as part of this process.

7. Write a phrase or something longer—an evocative description of something you experienced or maybe just a few words that came to you while you were moving.

8. Turn the process into a more polished creative project if you want, imagining what medium would best express what you experienced.

9. Reflect on whether the thoughts and feelings that came up remind you of any situation in your life, and whether you learned anything from this process that might apply to that situation.

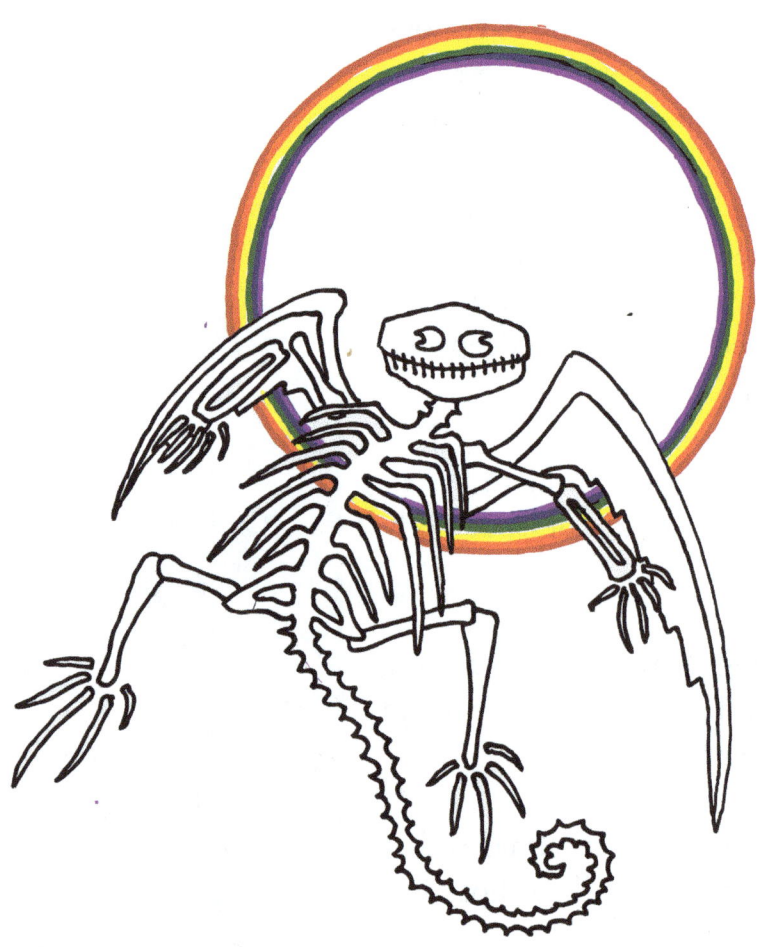

This image of a dead lizard, which relates to a personal experience I hadn't considered in a while, came up for me while using this method. It helped me to reframe those memories, while also creating a visually interesting piece of work. This is not the sort of thing that would normally occur to me to set out to draw!

SPELLCASTING PART 3: CREATIVE RITUAL

Balancing the elemental energy in your life can lead to greater satisfaction and feelings of ease as you flow from one situation to another. I hope that as you work with these ideas and exercises you will start to notice these effects, plus an uptick in surprising coincidence and moments that feel more magical. Starting to invoke this kind of magic in your life can feel like an uphill battle at times, though. We're all so heavily enculturated to believe that it's not going to happen.

On some level, this kind of enculturation is unavoidable. In order to have any kind of embodied existence at all, we have to have some understanding of who we are and who we aren't, how things work and how they don't. This is the kind of basic structure that allows us to function at all on a day to day level, communicating with others on the basis of certain common assumptions (including, for example, how words work, how money works, where each of us lives, which direction is up, etc.) The content of these assumptions is not so much true as it is necessary—there are many functional ways of relating to others and the world, but having to work out the answers to all these questions at every moment and in every interaction is pretty much impossible.

The process of becoming more magical allows us to inhabit these useful structures a little more fluidly, though. As we broaden our options and start to chase down more of our dreams, we start to understand that, while we can't opt out of this kind of definition entirely, we can learn to shift and re-shift its boundaries. Like hermit crabs, we can get up and walk out of any structure that no longer fits, trusting our intuitive nature to find us something at least a little bit better in this moment.

Making the space to make these changes, somewhat outside the normal order of things, is an important function of ritual. According to one definition, a *ritual* is just a particular, predictable way of doing something. When we talk about ritual in the context of spirituality, though, we generally mean something more like a sacred event. *Sacred* is harder to define than *ritual*, but the root of the word means set apart. Set apart,

generally, for God or for religious purposes, but there's something paradoxical about this setting apart. What really makes something sacred? Sometimes there are cultural signs that one thing is more likely to be sacred than another, but the main thing is that they're set apart by this naming, the sacredness itself being spoken into being.

That is, a *holy* site is a site that someone has decided—for supernatural reasons or otherwise—to regard as holy (although interestingly, while *sacred* and *holy* generally function as synonyms, the root of the word holy actually refers to wholeness, rather than separation). A sacred ritual is a space in which participants agree (more or less) that whatever happens in that time and place is more sacred than average, and so that place and time are set apart, fundamentally, by nothing other than this self-declared sense of sacredness. There's often a ritual involved, but importantly it's not the ritual that creates the sacredness (having your morning coffee can be a ritual, but that only makes it sacred if you say it does). What the ritual often does is communicate to everyone involved, on a subconscious level, that the rules operate differently in this space. These aren't iron-clad rules about behavior, but more like subtle changes in those prevailing social agreements—in particular, the common subconscious agreement that most of what we're doing most of the time isn't particularly sacred or magical.

So, the decision to make a particular time and place sacred is at the root of spiritual ritual. Behaving in different ways in that space—for example, dressing differently, speaking in hushed tones or with dramatic flair, moving in prescribed patterns and so on communicates to your intuitive mind that things really are going to be different here. Of course, acting in these atypical but repetitive ways, as well as using additional sensory stimuli like music and scent also tends to lead to a light trance state, which in turn is extremely conducive to a sense of spiritual experience (and, in many cases, drastically improved magical results).

Every time you experience this set-apart space and state of mind, you vividly demonstrate that the everyday rules really are pretty malleable. With any luck, when the ritual ends and you return to your normal state of mind, your *normal* will have shifted just a bit in the direction of your dreams.

ON CASTING CIRCLES

"With a ring of wave and rain and tears
I encircle this sacred space and all within.
Let nothing enter unwelcome."

— Yasmine Galenorn, *Embracing the Moon*

Wiccans, in general, think a lot about sacred space; other Witches, maybe not so much. This might be partly because a lot of solitary Witches are used to passing in and out of magical states of mind without any particular need for ceremony or group coordination, and partly because of the whole diversity of practice thing. Groups of Witches may wish for ways to access sacred space together, but need to be creative about it because there's less obvious shared vocabulary of ritual. This is a case in which I feel very comfortable borrowing from Wiccan tradition, especially because it involves the elements. There's still a lot of variation from one group or practitioner to another, but this is the way I cast a circle when I want to give a spell or group activity a little extra oomph.

The basic idea is that you choose a circular space, possibly preparing it ahead of time by marking a physical circle somehow. You can also cleanse the space with herbal smoke, or anything else you want to do to make the space feel more magical. It should be big enough for all of the people involved and all the activities taking place to fit inside. When you're ready to get started and everyone is assembled, take a few deep breaths and relax your mind. Tune in to your body, feeling the energy flowing through you (you can do the energy ball exercise if it helps you get in touch with this feeling). For group rituals, you can lead everyone through some or all of these steps, or let one person deal with the casting.

When you're ready, walk to the east edge of the circle, facing out. Hold up your hand or a tool like a knife (for marking clear boundaries) or wand. Speak to the power of air, inviting it to join you in the circle, then walk around the circle clockwise. Use your hand or tool to "draw" a line of energy around the circle, imagining it as a protective ring made of wind and clouds.

Continue, past the point where you started, to the south edge of the circle. Repeat the process, calling on the element of fire and drawing a ring of fire and light around the area. In the west, call on the power of water and visualize a ring of water and mist, then finish in the north by calling on earth and imagining a boundary of crystal or stone. You can, of course, call the elements in a different order if that feels right to you, but make sure to complete at least one full circle for each element rather than leaving gaps. Wiccans also tend to invoke gods and goddesses after finishing the circle, and this is a good time to call on any additional spirits that you want to invite to your ritual.

The space inside the circle is said to be between the worlds, meaning that it's not fully part of the everyday world or fully part of the spirit world. You can cast spells, meditate, practice trance or do creative work inside. When you're done, reverse the process, thanking any spirits you invited, walking to each corner of the circle to thank the element in that direction and then walking around the circle counterclockwise as many times as you walked clockwise before. Use your hand or other tool to unwind the layers of energy that you previously wound.

If you still feel full of energy when you're done, you might want to put your hands on the ground and release anything extra to the earth. Eating or drinking something is another good way to ground yourself, and a popular way of ending rituals.

ON RITUAL AND PLAY

Many people who are attracted to Witchcraft, especially in its more creative and personalized forms, also happen to be highly allergic to structure. There are probably a few reasons for this. For one, a lot of structure tends to be handed down with dogma, like the idea that we have to do something in a certain way because God said so. (Ironically, it's very possible that the dogma got attached to the practice in the first place because the practice was so good and effective that somebody at some point was trying to use the dogma to get people to try it, but the bottom line is that it tends to happen.) If you've dismissed the dogma, sometimes it makes a certain amount of sense to dispense with the ritual, too. On the other hand, we sometimes toss out the ritual exactly because there *isn't* a justification behind it. If people have been doing something in the same way for a long time without any known reason, that can be pretty easy to dismiss, too.

And, especially if you're practicing alone, ritual probably isn't *strictly* necessary. You can just decide one morning that your coffee *is* sacred and your car is a magical chariot and wherever you get out is a gateway to the spirit world and you can see how that works out. It's even somewhat possible to do this kind of work in groups, especially if everyone has a strong intention to share a magical experience and ideally a bit of practice slipping in and out of trance states without help (hint: try this with a bunch of artists).

Let's say, though, that you want to experiment, maybe in a group, and you could use a little more guidance. I struggled with this for a long time, until I noticed a really interesting thing: there are definitions of sacred space and definitions of play that are really, really similar, and I don't think that's a coincidence. Just like sacred space, *play* is often a situation where the "rules" of a certain time and place are changed, ideally by the agreement of everyone involved. For example, the temporary agreement might be that one person is a dragon, or nobody can cross a certain invisible line, or that whoever gets the most points (whatever those are) wins.

Again, it's not the specifics of the rules that create the magically playful quality of events, it's the shared commitment to engaging on those different terms. Curiously, like spiritual experience, play seems to be a built-in function of the human animal that we do spontaneously to learn, build relationships, process emotion and generally maintain healthy homeostasis. I actually feel pretty strongly that this similarity should not be overlooked. It might not even be too much of a stretch to imagine that spiritual and creative practice are both—ideally—adult versions of child's play, and that the entire process is intended to serve a naturally central, healing and magical role throughout our lives.

In practice that could unfold in so many different ways, but one idea that I love for a less structured group process is a bring-your-own-rules ritual. I do think that it works best if everyone agrees to a shared intention to create sacred space at the gathering. Then, each person comes up with a guideline to contribute. For example: *everyone wears green*, or *let's all bring flowers to put on an altar*, or *we'll take turns drumming quietly while everything else is happening*. Or, you know, *let's pretend one person is a dragon*—don't be afraid to get too weird. Then, just try to improvise. Unless something happens that makes someone really uncomfortable, I think the principle of *yes, and* is really helpful here. In theatrical improvisation, this is the idea that your scene won't usually get very far if one person says that they're in a restaurant and the next person says that they aren't. In that spirit, if something unexpected happens, try to go with it and be creative about where you could go from there.

I do think that especially if you're new to this, it's a good idea to have some sort of main event pre-planned. Just like you could with a more formal ritual, you could segue into some kind of meditation, spellwork or sacred conversation on a particular topic. It's also good to be aware of when you're leaving the ritual space, so keep some ideas for formally closing things out in the back of your mind.

ON SYNCHRONICITY

Besides rapid progress toward your goals there's a particular thing that tends to happen when you invite more magic into your life, and that is meaningful coincidence. Psychologist Carl Jung (who, like Crowley, did some upsetting stuff but was nonetheless a huge influence on modern occultism) called it *synchronicity* (literally, things happening at the same time). Jung's classic example occurred while he was working with a patient who was too attached to rational thought to cope well with her feelings. One night she dreamed of a rare golden scarab beetle, and the next day her therapy session was interrupted by the surprising arrival of the same type of beetle in Jung's office. In short, you could think of synchronicity as the way that symbolism sometimes shows up in real life.

Synchronicity is a bit hard to define because there's always a rational explanation as well as a magical one. There was a logical reason, however odd, that that beetle was in that office at that time. The fact that there is, technically, a real-world explanation for why something is possible doesn't disqualify it from being magical, though. With a bit of practice, you'll know it when you see it and notice that incidences of synchronicity tend to pick up dramatically when you're involved in magical work. They're usually a sign that more material results are on the way, and are also well worth watching in their own right.

When synchronicity occurs, I would strongly recommend working with it in the same way that you could work with a night-time dream. For example, if I were that patient with the beetle dream, I might have created a scarab painting or gotten some kind of scarab amulet to wear to invoke the memory of that situation and continue being present with its meaning.

Another thing I sometimes like to do is keep a journal of synchronicitous and magical moments. This is kind of like a gratitude journal and a magical record book lumped together, except I draw little pictures of everything which makes it more fun. Plus, I actively look for things that could possibly be considered evidence that magic is at work in my life. So, I have lots of pictures of interesting dreams, natural wonders and magical stuff to flip through, which comes in handy when I'm waiting for spell results.

CORE PRACTICE: TRANCE

Another great way of getting in touch with your subconscious mind is through trance. The conscious mind is by definition associated with normal states of consciousness, so all altered states—to one degree or another—create more direct access to the subconscious. Dreaming is a great place to start, but it has some drawbacks. Most importantly, we tend to do it when we're sleeping, and few of us have a significant amount of control over our nighttime dreams. Trance is kind of a middle ground—a bit like dreaming and a bit like being awake—and thus very useful for working directly with the contents of the subconscious.

Beyond that, trance is actually very hard to define. It's sometimes associated with a physiological state of deep relaxation, but high-energy trance is also possible. Since both words are incredibly hard to pin down, it's hard to say for sure if trance is precisely the same thing as hypnosis, but the two states do seem to have a lot in common. While some people think of hypnosis as a sort of mind-control, modern practitioners tend to understand that it's really a pretty normal state of consciousness that we slip into and out of all the time.

This mysterious state has a quality of feeling deeply absorbed in one thing. The most interesting thing about it might be that the critical faculty (the part of the mind that judges whether things make sense or not) is temporarily bypassed. Suspension of disbelief while watching a movie is an example of a natural trance. Not only do you watch the action unfold without constantly thinking about whether it's real or not, but you may actually respond viscerally to what's going on on screen by laughing, crying or jumping in your seat when something startling happens. These things don't happen because you believe that the story is true, but because you've allowed it to connect directly to your body and subconscious mind, *as though* it were a real situation.

You can also pay attention to the way that you slip in and out of trance while watching the movie. Maybe you snap out of it temporarily because you're hungry or uncomfortable or reminded of a situation in real life, but then you start to pay attention again and drift back in. We go in and out of trance like this all the time, during almost every type of activity. There's even some evidence that we naturally slip into a trance-like state whenever we're about to make an important decision.

In a trance state for magical purposes, it's possible to apply this kind of concentration and transformative capacity—possibly at an even deeper level—to situations that you imagine on purpose. We've already discussed the power of visualization, but visualization, intention setting and symbolic ritual may be even more effective in a trance state, where they can be introduced directly into the subconscious.

Meditation is a type of trance state, but in order to work with imagery, the concentration on the breath must be exchanged for concentration on something else. You can start to practice in a similar way, though. Sit in a comfortable meditation posture or lie flat on your back (a very relaxing position can help to facilitate a deep trance, but if you find that you fall asleep easily you may have to try something else). Some people find it helpful to listen to repetitive drumming or another type of relaxing, non-distracting music.

Close your eyes and mentally scan your body, starting with your toes and taking a second or two to focus on each area and invite it to relax deeply. After you relax all the obvious parts you can go through and check in on the internal parts, too, like the bladder, intestines, stomach, lungs, heart, tongue, and eyes. Finish with the mind, imagining that it's like a gently rippling lake becoming completely still as you relax.

After that, two common techniques are to count backwards, pausing occasionally to remind yourself that you're going deeper and deeper into a relaxing state, or to start to imagine some sort of scene where you're physically descending—maybe down into a cave or down a set of stairs—symbolizing the descent into the depths of the subconscious.

My personal favorite is to finish the full-body relaxation with the peaceful mind-lake, then imagine jumping into the lake, finding it perfectly natural and comfortable to swim deeper and deeper into the water. After vividly imagining this for a few minutes (I'd normally suggest bringing in as many different senses as possible, but imagining smelling underwater can get complicated) I'll visualize a door at the bottom of the lake, leading to whatever kind of magical place I want to be.

Once you memorize at least one induction process like this, it becomes pretty second-nature. If you're new to trance, though, you might want to ask a friend to stay conscious and guide you through the process, or use a recording to remind you of the steps. Some people worry that they could get stuck in trance, but as it's a natural state that we pass through all the time, there's no reason to worry about this. You'll decide to return to normal consciousness at some point unless you fall asleep, in which case you'll eventually wake up as usual.

ON SPIRIT GUIDES AND POWERFUL PLACES

There are many magical uses for the trance state. For example, some practitioners report the ability to move their awareness through the world in a sort of spirit flight to see, hear and otherwise participate in activities they would normally find impossible based on their physical limits. This is worth experimenting with, but is probably a more advanced sort of thing that might come with a lot of experience. More common trance-based practices include visiting unreal—that is, imaginary or else simply not of this world—locations, usually to learn useful lessons and sometimes meet spirit guides.

This is a practice that I highly recommend experimenting with. After entering a trance, tell yourself that you're about to enter an extremely comfortable, extremely powerful place. Imagine passing through a doorway of some kind, and see what you find. You may need to remind yourself several times that there's no wrong way to do all this—you may step through that doorway and find an entire scene unfolding around you, or you may have more of a feeling that you're consciously thinking of ideas and adding them to the scene. Either way is fine, but do try to make space for surprising intrusions, which sometimes lead to the most insight.

Orient yourself in your trance-space. This may be a place that you want to build up over time, revisiting it whenever you need to do trance work. If you want to, you can ask a spirit who would like to help you with your magical studies (or anything else you need help with) to appear.

Spirits can take an almost infinite number of forms. Common types include animals, spirits of place, angels, daemons, gods and goddesses, ancestors, fairies and even aliens, but the possibilities are pretty much unlimited. If someone or something does show up, be polite and have a conversation (which, by the way, may take place in imagery or some other form rather than words) about how you might be able to help each other.

As with human relationships, you don't have to take what you're offered. If you don't get a good feeling from the spirit or aren't interested in what it has to say, feel free to walk away (and end the trance, if you feel at all uncomfortable). The most fruitful spirit partnerships generally develop over time, though, so be sure to ask whether there are particular offerings you should make or other practices you should take on if you want to keep working with this spirit in the future.

Most people who go looking for this kind of spirit contact will find it pretty easily. If you don't, the most likely explanation is that what's showing up isn't matching your expectations. When I walk someone through a trance to meet a helping spirit and they don't see anything at first, my next question is, "if you did see a spirit coming to help you right now, what would it look like?" The imagination is an important part of working with the imaginal realm, and almost everybody is able to make contact when they think about it that way.

As I mentioned in the section on altars, there are a lot of different opinions on exactly how all this works on a spiritual level. According to some traditions, there are literal realms you can explore, map and revisit, and any number of different classes of spirit you can work with in different ways. I think it's worth exploring some of these traditional cosmologies (I'm partial to the somewhat Norse-inspired idea of a weird but fertile subconscious-

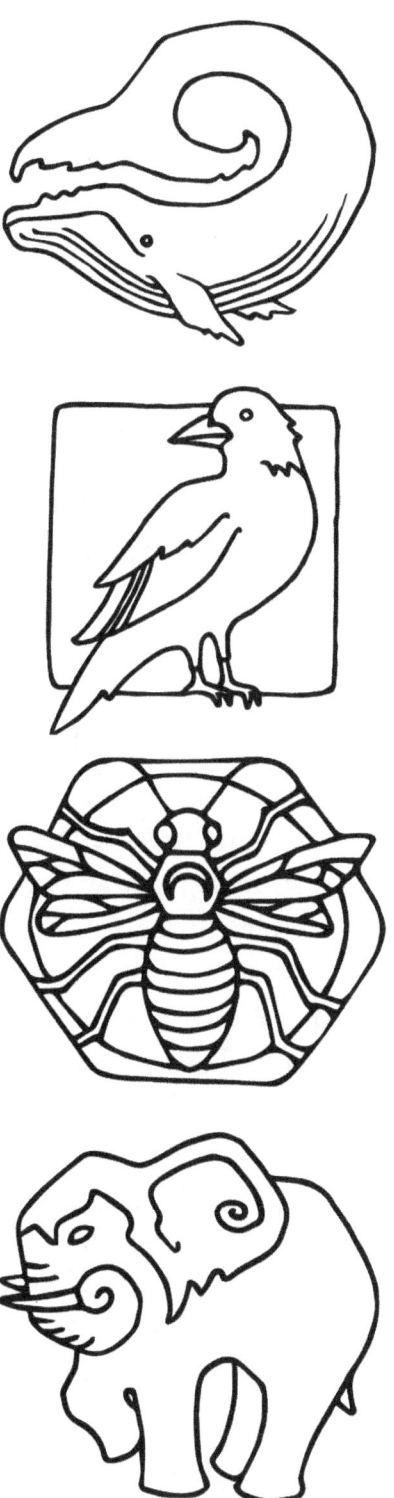

like underworld and an overworld of clear ideas and ideal beings, connected by a central world-tree).

There's another perspective that this is all just a way to communicate with your own intuitive wisdom, though, which I also think has at least a bit of truth to it. Whatever the ultimate nature of the beings involved, it's certainly true that what you see is somewhat influenced by your subconscious ideas and expectations. I guess my professional opinion is that Witchcraft neither requires nor necessarily imparts the ultimate truth of this sort of question, but one does tend to gain greater proficiency and trust in the process with practice.

ON CULTURAL APPROPRIATION (PART 2)

The English word *shaman* comes from the German *Schamane*, which has been in use since the mid-1600s but seems to derive, by way of Russian, from the Siberian tribal word šamán, meaning the magic-workers in that area. It's possible that this word, in turn, originally came from a Chinese word for a Buddhist monk, which is a vivid demonstration of the way that language and spiritual practices tend to spread, together and separately, through the world in various directions.

In modern times it has gotten pretty common to use the word *shamanism* to describe the magical practitioners of indigenous tribes all over the world. There are certain spiritual practices (including trance and communication with spirit guides) that tend to be common among these traditions, though the practices do vary widely and significantly in context and specific details.

At times, people who are not indigenous also use the word *shamanism* to describe their practice, particularly if they focus a lot on animism (interacting with the spirits of plants, animals and objects), healing and visionary states. While I think an argument could be made that the word *shaman* legitimately migrated into European languages centuries ago, it's worth noting that it wasn't used by Germans at that time to describe their own practice.

Outside of historical context, *shaman* has meant something specific in modern times, and that something has to do not only with spiritual practice but also with a network of community relationships and direct transmission of traditions within that community. If you aren't part of a traditional, community-based lineage like that—even if you do spiritual work for your community—that difference in context matters. Using words like *shaman* to describe yourself if you don't have that kind of lineage blurs those important distinctions and (ironically and however well-intended) contributes to ongoing erasure and misunderstanding of living indigenous traditions.

The same pretty much goes for related bits of language that are creeping into the spiritual mainstream, like *spirit animal* and *smudging* (a particular way of burning sage to purify something). Although these are both English words, they have a historical association with Native American practice, specifically, which gets muddied when people in non-native traditions start to use them for their own purposes.

This goes for all usage, but at least double for saying things like, "root beer is my spirit animal." If your argument is that you really need these words for your sacred practice, you probably know that this kind of thing makes that argument all the more ridiculous. I'm all for taking spiritual practice lightly, but that gets dicey when the tradition you're taking lightly is neither your own culture's nor a major power—like the Christian church—in mainstream culture.

In any case, the idea of contacting and forming partnerships with archetypal animal spirits (or, for that matter, burning herbs for magical purposes) is common all over the world, but people all over the world have historically described these practices in their own terms, and many Native Americans have asked white people in particular to continue doing so. One thing we could really use more language around is the idea, implied by shamanism, that the role of the artist and the spiritual practitioner are fundamentally the same. In general, though, we do have plenty of our own words for magical powers (and by "our own" I mean common to the English-speaking world, though you may find some more useful words in specific cultural traditions relevant to you). One of my personal favorites is Hedge-witch, which means a Witch specializing in boundary-crossing and trance states. Animist is another handy, non-appropriative word.

For animal magic I like talking about things like Owl Power (this reminds me pleasantly of superheroes) or dreaming Horse Dreams. Historical Witches used to have *fetches* and *familiars* (yes, these words had pretty specific connotations, in context—but if that worries you and talking about spirit animals doesn't, that's probably worth a second look). Some Harry Potter fans have suggested *patronus*. If you don't like anything else you can find, there's definitely something to be said for creating new language for the brand new thing, extra-specially particular thing you want to speak into being. Ask the spirits you meet what *they* want to be called, or make something up yourself. You don't need to use a particular word to make it count.

ON HEALING SPELLS

Healing is a popular topic in magic, and there are a lot of different ways to approach it. Simple spells are fine, as usual. If your interest is in healing someone else, your best bet is usually to light a candle with the intention of healing for their highest good and then get on with supporting them in whatever *their* process is. This is because healing is such a highly personal and individual sort of thing.

For your own healing, besides spellwork you could consider energy work, herbal remedies and of course lifestyle interventions like making sure you're eating, moving and sleeping as well as possible. This isn't to say that you shouldn't seek more conventional treatment—that's a very personal and nuanced decision—but there's hardly any situation in which natural therapies can't make some sort of positive difference regardless of what else you choose.

If you do work with holistic therapies, keep at it for a while. We're pretty accustomed to feeling better or at least different soon after taking a pill, and natural methods can be powerful but rarely work as fast. If you change your diet or start drinking an herbal tea, it might take a month or more to really notice significant changes.

In the meantime it's also really good to work with your intuition, because even very real medical issues often have significant psychological or spiritual roots. One thing to try is to think of your symptom as an ally and ask it what it's trying to tell you—this can be a useful journal exercise.

I also really like using trance for health issues. Try lying down comfortably and using your favorite method to go into trance. When you feel really relaxed, think of your main symptom and allow yourself to notice it in your body. Ask yourself what the symptom would look like if you could see it, and allow an image to come to you. Examine the details of the image. Does it remind you of anything? Does it tell you anything about what might be going on? Give this process plenty of time, but when you're ready, ask for an image of perfect health. How is that image different from what you're currently experiencing? Finally, imagine what it would be like for your image of discomfort to transform into the image of health. How would the change take place? Slowly? Quickly? Is anything needed to help this transformation along? Tell yourself that this transformation is happening right now, in your body, and notice how you feel as that happens.

Repeat as often as you like, and try to remember any powerful images to incorporate in future creative projects and rituals.

ON DREAMS

It's certainly possible and a good idea to work directly with images from your nighttime dreams, too. This was a big deal for the surrealists, which I have to admit kind of put me off of the idea for a while. There's obviously a lot of skill involved in those paintings, but I always felt a bit bored with the apparent randomness. It took me a while to notice that that's the opposite of how actual dreams (at least the interesting ones) feel to me on the inside. Dream symbols may seem random from the outside, but the really cool thing about them is the sense of numinous meaning. When an artist can convey that kind of sensation it's actually quite amazing, and we should probably thank the surrealists for that since popular culture wasn't paying a lot of attention to dreams before their time.

If you want to work with your own dreams, a good place to start is with a dream journal. It could be a section of your magical notebook, or a small book you keep by your bed all the time. When you wake up, before doing anything else, write down whatever you can remember about your dreams. If you can't remember anything, get out your notebook anyway and write a little about how you feel and how you slept. After starting this practice, most people remember more of their dreams pretty quickly.

If you have a particular question you can hold it in your mind as you fall asleep, intending to receive a message about it in a dream. When you write about your dreams, pay a lot of attention to your feelings and random associations. Dream dictionaries that give interpretations of common symbols are available, but since dreams are so personal, what something symbolizes for you could be very different from what it means to someone else.

If you want to interpret your dreams, think about some detail that grabs your attention and ask yourself if it reminds you of anything in your life. You could do this as a journaling exercise, freewriting about whatever associations come to mind. One interesting way of thinking is that every character in a dream represents a part of yourself—so, you're yourself or the "hero" of the dream, but you could also be the person or situation causing you problems. Why do you think other-dream-you is doing this to yourself? Dream villains and other odd characters (even if they seem to be someone you know) can represent parts of yourself that you don't consciously identify with, which is an especially good window into things that might be going on in your subconscious.

And, of course, you don't have to interpret a dream in order to work with it magically. If you have a dream that feels especially powerful but you're not sure what to do with it, you could also consider painting it, getting friends together to act it out, writing a poem about it, using it as a starting point for a trance or seeking an experience that reminds you of something that happened in the dream. This might spontaneously lead to more conscious understanding, but it's also entirely possible to keep playing around with the imagery on an intuitive level until you feel like something has resolved and you're ready to move on.

Then, of course, there's lucid dreaming. This is the idea that you can learn to realize that you're dreaming without waking up, allowing for some degree of conscious control in the dream world. One good trick for this is getting into the habit of asking yourself whether you're dreaming frequently throughout the day. Once this becomes second nature, you'll eventually start to remember to check this even while you're asleep. You'll probably wake yourself up the first few times that you notice you're dreaming, but over time it becomes less surprising and easier to navigate. Once you're able to stay asleep, the possibilities are nearly infinite. For one thing, pretty much any magical exercise that can be practiced while awake can also be practiced while dreaming, which opens all kinds of interesting doors.

Opposite is a coloring page (created in collaboration with my partner, James) that you can use as part of a healing spell if you want. You can also download a printable version at http://lauragyre.com/creativerituals. Focus on your specific healing intention while coloring the image, then use it however you like to complete your spell.

MORE EXPERIMENTS WITH WATER

1. Drink more water, it's (probably) good for you.

2. Go swimming or boating, or visit a river or an ocean if you can. Go out in the rain. Allow yourself to feel deeply and reflect on the qualities of this experience.

3. Use herbal tea bags, non-toxic crystals, candles, fancy bath products or whatever you like to create leisurely baths for ritual cleansing and relaxation.

4. Make art about water. You might want to use ink or watercolor and splash around in it a little. Encourage yourself to sink into the process, have a playful approach and go with the flow.

5. Feed your intuitive mind a high-quality diet of inspiration. Make a point of surrounding yourself with art you love and reading stories that fill you with a sense of possibility, for example.

6. Create magical talismans. If you have a powerful dream or trance experience, consider crafting or otherwise acquiring a symbolic object that reminds you of the experience and connects you with its power.

7. Practice listening to your intuition, even when you aren't sure exactly what it's saying. Learning to trust it can take time, but try to follow through on any odd impulses that come up, especially if the consequences aren't likely to be severe. If you suddenly feel like trying a different route on the way to the grocery store, for example, why not do it?

We have a house rule around here: *you thought of it, now you have to do it*. I don't actually suggest following that rule religiously, but it can be fun to think about. See what happens!

8. While I was writing this section, I had a dream. A writer friend told me about a magical exercise: flip through a dictionary and randomly select a few words, then write a short story using all those words. My conscious mind isn't quite sure what to make of that one, but it seemed worth noting here—one final suggestion from my subconscious to yours.

IV. TURNING UP THE HEAT

This will be you some day, if you study and practice Witchcraft: you'll be going about your business lighting candles, collecting herbs and talking to spirits. Maybe you'll be with some friends getting ready to start a group ritual, or alone in the woods hugging trees. You'll be in the middle of something you've tried before, or similar to something you've tried before, and it will go according to plan. Except, suddenly you will feel like a total idiot.

This is, I secretly think, why witchcraft isn't even more common. Almost anyone who has dabbled in it can tell you interesting stories. I like to think that if you spend some time working through this book, you'll have stories of your own to tell (or not to tell—sometimes, talking about that awesome thing that happened to someone who isn't really ready to listen is one of the quickest routes to getting disenchanted yourself). As awesome as it will be, though, the magic you experience won't change everything completely.

You'll keep up with the practices, or you won't. Life will keep being life, and even if you're pretty consistent, well, magic is a lot of things, but consistent isn't usually one of them. There are reasonably consistent trends, but there's something fundamental about magic that insists on keeping it subjective. A lot of things won't be very dramatic, and at some point I promise you will start to forget how far you've come and maybe even wonder why you started down this path in the first place.

I also want to acknowledge at this point that the element of fire is where things get pretty experimental for me, too. If all this feels a bit less put-together than what I had to say about air and mental habits, that's probably because it is. I've been tempted to go through this section a few more times with a heavy editorial hand, but instead I'm offering it as is in the spirit of comfort-zone expansion. I hope you'll agree that what these thought experiments lack in polish, they make up for by going in interesting and potentially powerful directions.

I guess my point is, it's part of the process to keep showing up—or at least leave the door open while you take some time to focus on other things—especially at those points when you feel like an idiot and nothing is happening, or you can't quite figure out where all this is going anymore. You can't always rush these things, but if I start to feel like things are really dragging and I'd like to jump start another magical cycle, I often find that going back to the basic practices like daily journaling can start to shake things up a little.

I'm sorry I can't promise anything more dramatic than that, but I can pretty much promise that if you keep coming back to your practice again and again no matter what happens, eventually you'll know in your bones that any feeling of absence is temporary. You'll start to trust that the magic will be back when you least expect it, but it will never stop surprising you with its power.

ON VULNERABILITY

I'm a pretty big fan of Dr. Brené Brown's work. She's a researcher and storyteller who started looking into the role of shame in our social relationships. To her surprise, she discovered that the people with the most life satisfaction are those who are willing to show up with their whole selves, even at times when doing so requires a significant amount of emotional vulnerability. Vulnerability wasn't such a popular topic before she started talking about it, but in retrospect it does feel kind of obvious. We tend to admire the people who really put themselves out there, imagining brand new things, living vibrantly and finding ways to bring surprising depth to everyday interaction. That kind of vulnerability is…vulnerable, though. Being the person who goes for something first or brings the most sincere emotion to a situation can feel like a big risk sometimes. It's easy to worry that you won't seem enough of something—cool enough, smart enough, considerate enough or whatever.

When we think of our friends, we rarely judge them in these ways that we worry others might judge us. A lot of us do have an internal feeling that something in our lives isn't quite…*enough* enough, though—and, ironically, the thing that might actually be missing is this willingness to show up fully, regardless of the outcome. This is, I think, deeply valuable territory to investigate, and I'm always on the lookout for ways to explore it more. While it can't be forced and certainly shouldn't be pressured (it's worth keeping in mind that some of us have actually been subject to far more shaming, rejection and dismissal than others, and expecting everybody to show up and share whatever's in their heart isn't really fair if they didn't sign up for that) it is true that showing up with this kind of authentic expression yourself can often inspire the same in others.

I guess I'm just saying that you might feel really vulnerable as you have that what-am-I-doing-here-moment, and you might end up with a massive vulnerability hangover (as Dr. Brown calls it) afterwards. But in between—*between the worlds*—when you fully commit to operating by different rules and maybe other people end up joining in, it's no coincidence that that's where the magic often happens.

ON THE POWER OF THE SHADOW

In general, this part is the part about discomfort and what you can do with it. Depending on your life circumstances you may have the option to stay in more comfortable territory if you prefer. Navigating a dynamic balance between body, rational mind and subconscious can already be quite a trick, and on the other hand can lead to very interesting results. A person who mindfully tunes in to these three areas is likely to improve their physical and mental health, develop deeper and more honest relationships with others and flow through life with a good bit more pleasure, ease and synchronicity.

If you ever find yourself looking for just a bit more, though, the missing element might very well be fire. A major association with fire, in various forms, is power, and the thing about power is that it's usually at least a little bit scary. Of course, anything you can do and any skill you can practice brings a kind of power. The particular thing we're talking about here is how to get more power, if that's something you want. Power itself is sort of a taboo—just the idea of wanting more of it—but I think that on some level most of us (maybe even all of us) do. This doesn't necessarily mean that we want to control other people. If you just want to achieve more than you have so far in your life, you could think of that as a desire for power.

Uncomfortably, one of the major lessons of fire is that you often get more power by doing things that are hard and maybe even scary for you. You may have noticed this while working with the other elements: if there were any assignments that you particularly struggled with but completed anyway with all the conviction you could muster, you may have experienced something that felt like a breakthrough. Sometimes that's just breaking through a specific type of resistance and knowing that it will be easier to do that thing again next time, but a lot of the time it feels bigger than that, especially if the resistance you run up against is pretty big, too.

One particularly common challenge is that you may encounter uncomfortable emotions while doing inner work, specifically anger and fear. Sadness is another uncomfortable feeling that often comes up, but most of the time it tends to flow through us more naturally—maybe because we're often more willing to accept it as a part of life. For whatever reason, sadness doesn't seem to lead to as many weird blocks as anger and fear, especially if we allow ourselves some space to feel it when it comes up. To some extent, the same principle goes for anger and fear. Both of those feelings can be valuable in the right moment and can help us to stay alive, which we talked about a little in the section on trauma. Fundamentally, both are just powerful signals that something is wrong.

Anger is a red flag that we're feeling attacked or accidentally trampled on in some way and we might need to take action to strengthen our boundaries and stand up for ourselves. That can be a helpful impulse under the right circumstances, but like the bodily sense of trauma, the feeling of anger can stick around for a lot longer than it's useful and really eat up our energy (especially if we aren't able to avoid the thing that we're feeling angry about). Anger about past events can also make it tough—and sometimes there's an element of physical trauma involved here as well, but even just the feeling of anger about something that happened in the past can make it hard—to be fully engaged in the present. On a magical level, being stuck in the past can make it challenging to have the most constructive and powerful kind of focus on achieving our current desires.

Both anger and fear are fundamentally resistant emotions, concentrating our energy on what we think shouldn't have happened, or shouldn't be happening now. Fear is resistance to a possible future, rather than something that happened in the past. Situational fear can be a healthy impulse that keeps us safe in certain moments, but it can also create problems when it becomes a chronic thing. For example, chronic fear and anxiety can contribute to a variety of health problems and can certainly make it difficult to feel peace, happiness and excitement about trying new things. Energetically in either case it's often unhelpful to walk around full of resistance to a thing that has already happened, or to something that might not even happen in the first place.

On the other hand, denying that these annoying, persistent feelings exist can also cause problems. Disowned fear and anger generally just get stuffed down into the subconscious, which is both magically powerful and hard to consciously control. You don't want to dig up something that scares you, for example, deny how much it scares you and then have it come up all the time in your dreams for further processing. In the worst case, these unacknowledged feelings and our attempts to avoid them can even help to attract more of the kind of actual situations that scare us into our lives.

Witchcraft's answer to this problem in general is to go toward those things you might find scary or otherwise emotionally triggering, rather than away from them. There are, of course, levels to this, and I urge you to approach this section, especially, at your own discretion (as well as, if appropriate, with professional guidance). However, I do think this kind of work is worth at least considering for most people on a magical path, since it can have such a profound interaction with the rest of our work.

The basic principle of emotional triggering is being reminded of something from the past so vividly that it impacts you physically in the present moment. So, for example, if you think back to a time you ate pizza and your mouth starts to water, that memory is triggering a physical response. Usually, though, the response that we're talking about is an emotional response. The things we think of as feelings are actually a complex combination of thoughts and physical sensations. So, if someone starts to talk about something that's upsetting for you, you probably notice that you're feeling scared or angry because your body is being flooded with adrenaline and you might feel your heart pounding or some of your muscles getting tight, which is a reaction that's both entirely natural and also built up in a complicated way over a lifetime of experiencing upsetting things that remind you of other upsetting things that have happened in the past.

As normal as it is to have these complicated triggers, though (and again, there are levels—I want to clarify that I'm not talking about major trauma here) it's helpful to have less of them, because the minor ones get set off all the time—sometimes lots of times each day—and they make us do weird things. We react emotionally to patterns from the past, which sometimes move us toward situations that repeat those uncomfortable patterns, instead of acting in ways that really move us toward our current goals. Plus, being highly reactive just upsets and confuses us and wastes our energy, as well as the energy of other people in our lives.

So, basically, there's a tendency in Witchcraft to carefully move toward many of those triggers and find ways to explore them in order to defuse them. Sometimes modern Witches call this *shadow work* after the psychological concept of the shadow, but the general theme has been around for much longer than the field of psychology and is part of why Witchcraft is associated with spooky things like skulls and bats. The idea of contemplating our mortality, specifically (which is more or less the basis for most of our more specific fears) is a powerful, ancient and extremely witchy idea.

ON SHADOW WORK

In our cosmology where air can be mapped to the thoughts, earth to the body and water to the deep mind, we could say that fire corresponds to the shadow—basically, the parts of ourselves that we consciously reject or remain entirely unaware of (this concept of the shadow is another one that comes from Carl Jung, who did a lot of work in mysticism as well as early psychology). Basically, it's a set of qualities that we're pretty sure we don't have, even though some part of us actually does have them. Often, we reject these qualities out of fear.

You know the idea that when you dislike someone, it could be because they do something that reminds you of yourself? That's a quick way to get a feel for how this works. If you can think of someone you have a hard time with, or just a behavior you've encountered people doing that really, really bugs you, ask yourself whether it reminds you even a little bit of anything about yourself. Chances are you don't do exactly the same thing, but you might uncover a related desire or quality that you reject.

Personally, the first time I noticed this happening in my life was around food. I have kind of a complicated relationship with food, but for one thing I learned a lot of rules about it as a kid. One of them was that if someone offers you some food you should never take more than your share—and I don't mean in some kind of dire survival situation, but just a situation where it's polite and other people might want some, too. This is a reasonable guideline that makes total sense to me, intellectually, to the extent that I've attempted to pass it on to my own kids. But I also noticed at a certain point that it really drove me crazy if I was hanging out with somebody and they ate more than I thought they should, especially if it was something that I wanted, too.

When I tuned in to what was really going on with that, I started to catch my brain saying things like *Oh my god, why did that person eat three cookies? This is the worst! Now there aren't enough cookies for everybody—there might not be enough cookies for me! They probably don't care if I starve and die.* I'm not saying that I literally believed any of that, but I did notice that I felt pretty self-righteous and, in a way, personally attacked, even though most of me knows that's pretty ridiculous. The thing is, though, that I just had this personal rule I hadn't even noticed stuck in my brain, and it wasn't really doing anybody any good.

Eventually I also noticed that the world wasn't ending and that people who ate too many cookies still had friends and nobody was starving, and it started to blow my mind a little bit. I realized that this idea that I assumed was universal wasn't, and there were so many different ways of relating to those situations. Then I started eating extra cookies sometimes, and it probably made some people mad—which is totally reasonable, because everybody likes cookies. Breaking through these blocks doesn't mean that your actions don't have consequences, and if I were really worried that there wouldn't be enough to go around I could think of different ways to make sure I could help meet everybody's needs, like bringing extra cookies to the party.

For the most part, though, these things that can seem like huge deals in our minds just aren't, and nothing really needs to be done about them at all. I also noticed that I felt like a better friend after I started eating more cookies because I wasn't so quick to judge others. Who cares how many cookies people are eating? Now if I notice something like that I tell myself that everybody is probably doing what they want, and I usually feel pretty good about it.

I think this is a pretty interesting kind of experiment, so I think it's really worth paying attention to exactly what bugs you when you start to get annoyed at people. Are they too bossy? Too needy? Too negative? Too careless? Whatever it is might be a clue to a part of your personal shadow. As you investigate this, I would think less about whether you do the exact same behavior, and more about whether you feel like you *can't*. What would it be like if you acted like that, too? Why would you ever want to do that? How would it feel? What would people think? Would anything irreparably bad actually happen?

There's a lot of power tied up in these shadow selves. When they're not properly integrated they can cause a lot of problems in our lives, like distracting us from things we would rather be doing, causing unnecessary conflict with others or just quietly stopping us from getting what we want a lot of the time. We'll never get rid of our shadow aspects completely, because we need certain ideas about who we are and who we aren't in order to function. The more aspects we can make friends with, though, the more fluid and open to possibility we'll feel, the less annoyance we'll encounter in the world, the more genuine understanding we'll be able to extend to others and the more magically effective we'll be on a variety of levels.

Maybe most importantly, understanding and integrating our various selves and qualities more fully means that we'll be better able to focus and refine our goals rather than getting in our own way all the time. For example, if you think you want a relationship but there's secretly a part of you that feels like all that communication is a hassle, the part that's worried about the hassle absolutely counts in terms of your desires. The more you reject and ignore that thought and tell yourself that you absolutely do want a relationship, the more you'll be stuffing that other desire (the desire not to have that) back into your subconscious, where it continues to have a powerful energetic effect and might contribute to behavior that's doing the opposite of attracting love. Once you're aware of this pattern, you may be able to work through your communication issues and let them go. On the other hand, you could also just focus your desire more precisely. In this case, maybe an intention to meet someone interesting and take things slowly might work out better than an intention to jump into a serious relationship.

There's no real way to get rid of unwanted shadowy bits of ourselves besides freeing them up and allowing them to evolve on their own if and when they're ready. The good news is that once they've been witnessed and met somewhat, they're often willing and ready to shift at least a little. So, what we want to do is just kind of allow them to surface, keep an eye on them, and understand that everybody has weird stuff in their brains and it doesn't have to define us. We all have many qualities, including qualities that might seem to be opposed to each other, like wanting to eat all the cookies and also wanting to share nice things with friends.

Another interesting thing about the shadow self is that it can actually include qualities we think of as positive, but still assume that we can't or don't have. So, for example, you might have a shadow quality of being kind, brave, charismatic or smart. Just like the qualities that seem less pleasant, we can also find ways to project these onto other people while we deny them in ourselves. If you think for a minute about someone or a quality you really admire and exactly what attracts you about that situation, it's pretty likely that you're attracted to a quality that resonates with you and your nature. That's a good sign that you have the ability to embody that quality, too, even if you haven't quite allowed yourself to feel it yet.

How all this works is pretty mysterious, but at times I have wondered *if it's so bad to shove those negative qualities down into our subconscious, couldn't it actually be good to shove some positive qualities in there, too?* And I guess that that might not be so bad, but it depends on what your goals are. If you keep telling yourself that you admire strength but you yourself can't be strong, then yeah, that might lead to manifesting more strength in your life—but probably externally. Maybe you'll manifest more awesome strong people in your life, but it's possible that you'll wind up feeling even less strong, yourself. On the other hand, if you're able to make more space in your life to at least acknowledge the possibility that you might also have the quality you admire, that paves the way for manifesting more of it in an internally embodied way—which is generally the most integrated and overall magically powerful way of manifesting.

A CURIOUS EXERCISE

A tricky thing about working with the shadow, of course, is that it's so deeply unconscious that it can often be hard to see at all. There can be certain signposts, like that irritation about someone else's behavior, or whatever it is that you're constantly jealous of when others have it. Occasionally, if you're open to it, someone who knows you very well might be able to point out something useful. I've also found this exercise from Catherine Shainberg really helpful. Her work is Kabbalistic, so she doesn't frame it in relation to the shadow, but in my experience it's a great way to dredge up interesting things you might not be aware that your conscious mind is avoiding.

The process is pretty straightforward. For three days in a row, write down everything and every quality you can think of that you like, love or are strangely attracted to. These are the things that you consciously identify with at least somewhat, and after three days of writing you should have a very long list. On the third day, reread all three lists. Then, drop your awareness into your belly and ask yourself *What's not on my list?* Pay careful attention to whatever comes up first. It could be a word, or it could be more like an image you'll need to investigate in order to get some answers. What is this thing that is strangely missing from your conscious identity?

Whatever that thing is, it's probably well worth your consideration. I've used this exercise repeatedly at different times, and each time integrating more of the missing quality has led to seriously interesting results and an increase in personal power.

ON POISON AS MEDICINE

In general, Witchcraft itself is deeply associated with power of all kinds—and while there are plenty of non-spooky sources of power, many of the most underutilized are underutilized for a reason. It's certainly fair to say that Witchcraft has a history of not shying away from spooky, taboo and generally strange ideas. Obviously, there's the part about facing your fears, up to and including the fear of death, and meditating on traditional witchy symbolism can certainly have its place in that process.

It's also worth noting that there's a long history of drug use in association with Witchcraft, as there is in many other magical traditions. People sometimes call this the poison path, though *pharmakon* might be a better word than poison. In ancient Greece, *pharmakon* meant poison, medicine and also magical spell, which is a mystery worth spending some time with. Whether the poison in question is a physical drug or a scary shadow aspect, it's definitely true that the dose makes the poison, and the roots of the transformation we most deeply need are often contained in the things that challenge us the most. When it comes to drugs, this is one of those things that's both literally true and also a metaphor.

Witchy herbs like Mandrake and Belladonna have hallucinogenic properties that are generally more dangerous than popular modern hallucinogens, but have been used in a similar way to facilitate and deepen certain types of trance and provide a relatively safe opportunity to come face to face with fears internally. Intense physical ordeals involving pain and deprivation have also been used for similar purposes. While we're close to the subject, there's also a significant historical association between Witchcraft and atypical or even taboo sexual practices, varying depending on context. Some of that is probably historical slander, intended to discredit folks caught up in Witch-based hysteria. Some of it touches on the real, though, in the sense that we're certainly aware that sex can induce altered states, that confronting the limitations of taboos can be empowering and that Witches certainly do seem to feel free to flaunt social convention when it suits their purposes.

All these practices can, in varying degrees, be scary, downright dangerous and at high risk of leading to abusive and/or addictive behavior (which is one way of describing the kind of stuck pattern that's pretty much the opposite of magical). Many people who are drawn to Witchcraft also have their own complicated history with this kind of edgework, ranging from instinctive harm reduction to problematic overcompensation. Still, in the context of informed adult consent, these poison-adjacent paths can sometimes be productive and even healthy to explore in a mindful way, subject to many of the same principles as any other type of magical practice.

It's also worth noting that this kind of exploration doesn't need to be an all or nothing sort of thing. For example, having a glass of wine or smoking a joint before a ritual is best to avoid as a crutch, but also a totally legitimate option. Personally, my favorite entheogen (a drug used to facilitate a spiritual experience) is probably coffee. I guess I'm just saying, if this kind of thing interests you, it's a highly individual path requiring a high degree of self-determination, but something simple like that is a fine place to start.

CORE PRACTICE: EMBRACING THE SUCK

This is, I hear, a military phrase, but I love the way it sums up an attitude of moving toward things we would generally rather avoid with a certain amount of gusto. In most cases, if you have an irrational or semi-rational fear, for example, it can be pretty freeing to confront it head on. That kind of process is never really over, but personally I went through a period of focusing on it intensely at one point in my life—doing things like eating bugs and signing up to go sky-diving—and it really did free up my energy amazingly. I try to revisit the idea from time to time, checking in on new fears as well as old ones that might still be hanging around, and in general I recommend it highly as a practice for increasing magical power.

If you want to try it, proceed at your own pace using your best judgement and armed with all the peace of mind, physical grounding and awareness of invisible allies that you've been developing. It shouldn't be easy but it should be pretty simple: just find some things you think you might be ready to face head-on (hopefully in a way that's not really too dangerous), and face them.

This could mean actually scary things, but it could also mean other kinds of challenge and discomfort that you generally go out of your way to avoid, like that one thing on your to-do list you've been putting off for over a year. If you can, try to face them all with a curious and playful attitude. Of course, you absolutely don't have to do these uncomfortable things, and they're not a requirement for Witchcraft. You might find that it changes a lot, though, if you can learn to want to sometimes.

ON FEAR OF FLUFF

But, I can almost hear you saying, what if you're not afraid of anything? What if you've already faced your darkest fears and emerged unscathed? First of all, congratulations—maybe fire is your element. There are a couple of points you might want to consider, though.

First of all, anyone can be a Witch, but realistically there are certain...cultural trends. Like, if you're anything like me, you wear a lot of black and really like going in the woods at night. If that reminds you of anybody you know, keep in mind that the challenging and scary thing isn't always the thing that seems dark and forceful, and vice versa.

It's true that Witchcraft has a strong association with spooky stuff and practices that are a little edgy. A lot of people are drawn to it for that reason, which is great if that works for you. There's a sort of reactive trend in parts of Witch culture, though, where we get so attached to being brave and way out there that we actually contribute to a kind of fear of nice, normal stuff, not to mention soft, awesome stuff. There's a tendency to write off huge swaths of practice—and the people who love it—as too fluffy or light-and-love or new age, with the implication that those people are at best misinformed and probably just too scared to do real, scary Witch stuff.

On one level I find this distasteful because I'd like to think we can agree that fluffy bunnies are a wonderful part of our magical ecosystem. I also find it kind of ironic because this judgemental attitude often sounds a lot like fear to me—possibly a fear of being seen as weak, stupid or maybe just boring. On the deepest level, I guess I mostly just find it sad, because being kind and loving is a beautiful thing and something that most of us want in our lives if we're able to be vulnerable enough to admit it. This is a bit of a pet peeve of mine, but I guess my point is that if you identify as a super scary Witch, it might be that the most difficult, severe, transformative practice for you would actually be to take it easy on yourself and then maybe post the top ten things you love about unicorns on your social media.

Mirror-world situations like that are a bit of an extreme example, but there are plenty of less obvious cases where the scary thing isn't really the scary thing. This isn't just based on your overall personality, but also on your particular situation in each moment. Almost anyone can probably think of a time when the challenging choice was to do the gentle, nurturing thing. And, for that matter, a lot of folks who could benefit from reading this message could also stand to give second and third thoughts to their relationship with tedious routine, too.

There are workarounds for many of the benefits of steady discipline, but the one thing they can't teach you is how to make do *without* those crutches and shortcuts. If you think there's an outside chance that you might be acting out some repetitive patterns about not letting anybody be your boss, maybe keep in mind that being your own boss at times might have its advantages. I guess I'm just saying, a fear of routine and discipline can also be a sneaky fear, and in my opinion that's an advanced-level fear that's well worth facing, too. What if you get bored? I know, the depths of that horror are almost unimaginable.

ON DISCIPLINE

While I think that personal discipline is well worth considering, I also find it to be a bit of a fraught topic in magic. People, especially the kind of men who tend to be attracted toward more rigid forms of ceremonial magic, sometimes like to tell other people who work more on the intuitive side that if you don't have discipline—basically, if you don't have a set of boring and time-consuming practices that you do pretty much every day—then you're not really doing magic or your magic will never be any good. I think there are a couple of things going on with this, but I have to admit that I say this as a not very disciplined Witch.

Discipline isn't a strong suit in any part of my life, and for what it's worth, my results can be impressive at times, but they can also be erratic—so maybe there's something to this thing about discipline. Also, though, there may be different ways of being successful with magic, and that all sort of depends on what you are going for. There are definitely a couple of useful things that can happen with disciplined practice. The first is just repetition. Meditating once is fundamentally not the same as meditating many times over the course of months or years, and some other practices just have to be done again and again in order to pay off, too. If you want to get a lot of repetition in, having a habit is a good thing. So if you want to get the benefits of meditation, I do think it's a really good idea to have a specific habit like sitting down for at least fifteen minutes every night before you go to bed, because the routine will help to remind you and prepare you mentally and just generally make the practice easier to do over time.

If you do want to build a habit, do whatever you can to set yourself up to follow through.

Get everything you'll need together, schedule time on your calendar or talk to friends so you'll have accountability, for example. In general, I like the idea of thinking about this kind of thing as a habit rather than a discipline because it's a more resilient framework. If one day (or one week, or one month) things get weird and you end up not doing your practice, then you've messed your discipline up. If it's just a habit, though, that's fine, and it's still a habit if you go back to doing it the next day, or the day after that.

So, discipline isn't necessarily better than habit for getting in a lot of practice, but it does do another interesting thing, which is give you an opportunity to do something difficult. On that one day that you really don't feel like meditating, it really might not be a huge deal if you skip it. On the other hand, this is a really good, really safe opportunity to practice pushing yourself a little. Pushing yourself to do things that feel somewhat uncomfortable is a skill in the sense that the more you do it, the less scary it will be, and the more practice you get at this skill, the more easily you'll be able to push yourself to do difficult things that actually could make a big difference in your life.

Of course, there are plenty of difficult things in life that aren't optional, but the idea is that if you have practice doing some of these things on purpose, the ones that come along outside your control will be easier to deal with. In some cases, you may even be able to avoid complications completely by addressing issues head-on instead of waiting for them to catch up with you. There are a lot of traditional spiritual practices along these lines, like fasting, or sleeping on the floor, or limiting yourself to a small number of possessions.

Like facing your fears, this sort of ascetic practice can be useful, but only to a certain extent. If you're able to do something of this sort occasionally in a limited way, with the attitude that you're building up power to confront difficult situations, you'll probably learn a lot about yourself and, yes, your discomfort-facing skills will improve. Sometimes ascetic practices can actually be damaging, though, especially if you have a history of being mean to yourself or others, or a significant history of discomfort you couldn't escape from even if you tried. So, apply with caution, and steer well clear of any system that teaches that everybody has to do this kind of thing whether they want to or not.

A totally disciplined practice doesn't usually feel like the best option for me, personally, for reasons of this kind. I do have a regular meditation habit, but some nights when it's time to do my practice I just feel tired and there's no spark at all about doing it. I can't avoid the hard work forever if I want to get the benefits, but I can choose to do it in a way that feels a bit more exciting. So, I may skip meditation for one night, but some other day I might take on something harder just because I feel up to it, like—to keep it consistent—an extra long meditation practice. In general, this is what I recommend: give yourself a break when you want or need to, but remember to do the opposite, too, and try something a bit out of your comfort zone when you feel up to it. Learn to keep your balance in motion, losing it a bit, then finding it again and again.

ON DOING THE HARD THING

If you do decide to pursue a difficult goal (occult, creative or otherwise), set yourself up for success. Think about what sort of plan has worked well for you in the past. You can hear all sorts of ideas that sound good in theory, but on some level you probably know what kind of method works well for you. Are you an all or nothing person, or do you like to ease into things gently? Does it help you get motivated to set things up in a fancy way and have a special environment with all the tools for your project prepared, or would you rather keep it simple and just grab a minute to work whenever you can?

One thing to keep in mind is the kind of magical resources we talked about in section two. When you're facing something you know will be a challenge, what makes you feel strong? Do you have some lucky charms you can keep around, or do you want to start by saying a prayer, reading something inspirational or putting on some music and/or an outfit that gets you in the right mood for your project? Having an accountability buddy or group is another kind of resource that I find really helpful sometimes.

Besides making everything as appealing and convenient as possible, the next thing I would suggest is just taking that first step. For example, when I'm feeling resistant to exercise I sometimes tell myself that all I have to do is get out my mat and stand on it, or maybe do five minutes of stretches. When I can do that much, I might just sit there for a few minutes, mostly to prove that I can trust that process—but probably ninety percent of the time once I get to that point it's easy enough to keep going and I can do it a little at a time, without a big commitment that feels scary.

There are a lot of things you could do in an incremental way like that, including the journaling. It's a really good idea to set a length or time goal because sometimes you'll feel like stopping just when you're about to get to the interesting part (Julia Cameron writes about the page-and-a-half-in truth point where writers often run out of daily trivia and get around to whatever is really on their minds) but if you're having trouble journaling at all I would still suggest getting out your notebook and writing even a sentence or two.

Bigger projects are often more complicated, but you can usually break them down into little steps. This might sound really obvious, but if you're feeling stuck on something you know you want to do, one way to jump in is by writing that list of steps. If listing all the steps still feels ambitious, just start with the first few. If even that feels daunting, you might need to break the items down even more, like: *brainstorm, write a list of questions I need to get answered, figure out who to contact about this, look up contact information, send an email.* Writing the list is actually the first step, but (like the gradual approach to exercise or journaling), once you have that list you may have an easier time moving on with the next couple of steps.

Tiny steps are really good, but honestly one of my favorite tricks for doing hard stuff is something I think of as a tiny step off a cliff. This is when there's a little, relatively easy thing you can do that pushes you past some kind of point of no return. So, for example, I mentioned that I signed up to go skydiving while I was facing some fears. I'm sure that the really hard, scary part of skydiving is the part where you're actually up in the plane, but once I was pretty sure that I wanted to try it I bought a ticket. Buying the ticket was kind of scary, but much less scary than the actual jump. In the end I waited at the wrong bus stop and missed the actual skydiving trip, but curiously just making that commitment really helped me get over my previous fear of flying.

They might not completely solve your problem, but those little steps with a big impact (which could also include announcing that you're about to do something, or physically traveling to the place where you'd like to do it) can make a huge difference if you're having trouble getting started. It's still technically possible to change your mind, but it's much less likely once you've committed some energy and resources to your intention.

THE EXTREMELY MAGICAL ONE HOUR DO-THAT-HUGE-THING-NOW PROJECT RITUAL

We all have that project. You know, the one you've been thinking about for months and also putting off for months, or maybe even years. If you're anything like me, you might even have more than one. Why haven't you started yet? No time? No money for supplies? Not sure how it's actually going to turn out, or how to even get started? These are all things I tell myself when I'm procrastinating, but they're not amazing excuses. Spending a little time is better than none, of course. Working with what you have is better than putting it off indefinitely. And, no, you don't know how it's going to turn out—you won't really know until long after you've started. If you don't start somewhere, though, it's never going to happen at all, and this is the problem, I think: it's just too big, too scary and too unknown.

The classic approach is to break the project down into tiny, manageable chunks. Make some lists. Do one thing at a time. There's nothing wrong with that, except that it's still kind of daunting. It might be a long list, and if you haven't started yet you might not even know what needs to go on the list. Also, it's kind of boring.

Here's a more exciting alternate method: *using only the materials you have on hand right now, start and finish your project in an hour.* This is the magic part—well, this and the fact that you're welcome to cast a circle first, and you might as well call on any relevant spirit guides. Then, jot your story down, write your book, paint your painting, record your song or movie or do whatever your big thing is.

This is, by the way, absolutely not intended to be an outline. The important thing is to finish the whole project. For example, the first time I tried this method, I made a one-hour book. I wrote it on paper, made a cover and bound it with yarn. You could turn your online class idea into a series of emails or a youtube video, get some paint on a big piece of paper, make a temporary dress with safety pins or record your song on an old tape recorder. Try to capture the most important details of your vision quickly, knowing that you will never, ever be able to get it all.

If your idea is so vague that you're still not sure where to start, just pick a place. It's only an hour, after all. Do as much as you can, with the understanding that you're in no way committed to this form for future work.

Did you finish? Hooray! Even if it took you a little more than an hour, that's an amazing accomplishment. It's ok if you hate what you made. Actually, it's pretty much supposed to be terrible—it's just also supposed to be done.

At least, sort of done. You now have a physical talisman of success, rather than a whole lot of nothing. You should also have a better idea of how the process might go, or at least which questions you'll need to ask to get started. Now you can write that list, keeping in mind that you know you can finish it. Or, if you want, you can give yourself an upgrade in terms of time and materials and repeat the process. In a way, you've already done the whole thing and you just need to see if you can do a little better next time. What does a five-hour book look like, or a one-day movie?

This is a sneaky and surprisingly effective way of working towards your big goals. My tiny book, in its second iteration, was a five-page pdf about this process that I give away for free. The third iteration was a bigger, illustrated paper zine about magic that got me my first book contract. The fourth version was a series of lectures on Witchcraft that helped me refine and expand the material, and the fifth version is the book you're reading now. Once you take the steps to get started, your project will work with you until you both figure out what it wants to be.

ON HARD THINGS THAT JUST HAPPEN

Doing hard things is all very well, of course, but then there are the other kind of hard things that show up suddenly, whether we want them to or not: misunderstanding, conflict, disappointment, annoyance, worry, boredom and so on. As long as these things keep showing up in your life, you can use them as fuel for your fire practice, too.

When moderately uncomfortable feelings come up, get a little space to process them if you can. If it feels workable, start by revisiting the body meditation. Rather than getting into the story of what you're upset about or pushing the feelings away, just allow yourself to experience the physical sensation and pay attention to how it shows up in your body. Notice, too, whether any images appear in your imagination when you focus on that physical sensation—especially creative, unusual images that may feel unrelated to the problem at first. You'll probably notice that the sensation in your body is really fluid and might change a lot. If the situation you're reacting to is kind of a big deal, the feelings may come and go more than once, which can be interesting to witness. This exercise is just about the power of paying attention, without needing to change anything.

Of course, this doesn't mean that you shouldn't try to resolve your problems. If a situation is upsetting you, you might still want to have a conversation about it, make personal changes, set firmer boundaries or even seek outside support—but you can do all that just as well (if not better) once you've gotten a deeper sense of your own emotional and imaginal response.

If you have more time, you can also work with this kind of situation by journaling. As a fire practice, keep journaling, with a special effort to do freewriting when you notice uncomfortable emotions. Prompts to try at this point include *I'm afraid... I'm angry about...* and *I would rather not think about...* Keep in mind that writing something down doesn't turn it into the immutable truth, and if you're really uncomfortable you can always burn the paper to release the energy when you're done.

ON MERCY AND SEVERITY

So, self-discipline and ambitious projects are magical, but gentleness and luxurious indulgence are, too? This can feel a bit like a paradox and occultists think about this one a lot, so there's special language for it. We usually call this polarity *Mercy and Severity*, which comes through Jewish mysticism and the Kabbalah. The Tree of Life diagram is often drawn with a black pillar called the pillar of severity on the left, and a white pillar called the pillar of mercy on the right (which is why you often see black and white pillars like that in tarot cards and other magical scenes). Mercy and severity refer to the powers of creation and destruction that work together to make the universe as we know it possible.

Life and death is one way to think about this polarity, though within the scope of our lives we might recognize it on a more personal level as growth and limitation. Limitation doesn't sound so great, but fundamentally it's limits that make each thing what it is instead of just part of a universal stew. On the other hand, growth sounds pretty good, but sometimes we're scared of that, too—especially because we've seen so many cultural examples of things that grow too much and with too little consideration for others. We need to find creative ways to come to terms with both of these powers in order to reach our full magical potential, though.

A lot of occult philosophy relates to finding some kind of balance between these two poles. One traditional idea was to strengthen a middle pillar between the two extremes (sometimes called the pillar of mildness). If you want to get more witchy about it, you could think about a lightning bolt or a crooked path, bouncing back and forth between the two extremes. In any case, cultivating harmony between these forces in our own lives is possibly *the* major challenge and the crux of occult practice. It's also one of those fractal ideas that shows up in so many different contexts. The rhythm of the breath, for example, is an embodied experience of expansion and contraction that most of us seem to manage effortlessly, and maybe this kind of grace in motion is an important lesson we can learn from studying the breath.

The poles of severity and mildness are also sometimes mapped to masculine and feminine qualities, specifically the qualities of being active and passive or receptive. This particular duality gets a lot of attention in magic, especially in Wicca where the sexual dynamic between Goddess and God is seen as a central mystery. When Wiccans use the map of the elements in the four directions, they often add an up/down axis, assigning a sky god to up and an Earth goddess to down. I've never felt entirely comfortable with the gender essentialism that tends to get lumped into that system, but I love the idea of mapping this central polarity of expansion, contraction and the space between the two.

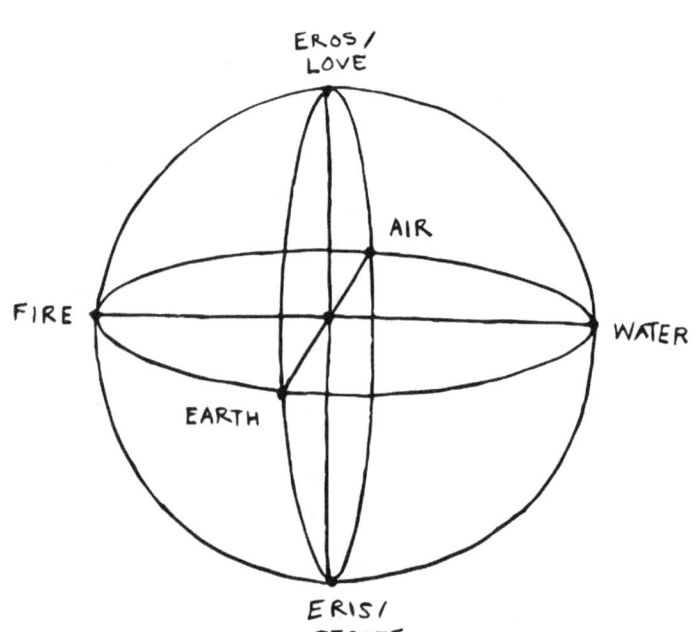

I was amazed and delighted when I started to research the ancient Greek roots of the elemental system and learned that Empedocles himself had also included the up and down directions in his original elemental map. He called them Eros and Eris (often translated as love and strife), for the god of sexual love and the goddess of chaos or discord. This is technically a god and goddess pairing, but it feels like Empedocles was pointing pretty specifically to the dynamic tension between generative organization on one hand and disintegration on the other.

Curiously (or maybe not), I've also caught glimpses of this dynamic at the intersection of chaos theory and evolutionary biology—subjects I won't pretend to understand very deeply, but enough to appreciate the parallel that just as biological life thrives with the most diversity at the borders between ecosystems, it also thrives in a precise, dynamic balance between order and chaos. If there's too much order, there's no variety and too little ability to adapt to changing conditions. Too much chaos and, of course, the biological system ceases to be a system.

This zone of thriving between the two extremes seems to be pretty central to human nature as well, so, of course, it's only natural that magical practice pushes us toward it. Remember the hot air balloon? You don't entirely control the direction, but only whether you want to go higher or lower to catch the wind. Personally, I think of this kind of calibration between mercy and severity as the way we control the heat. How much fire do you need right now? Where are you trying to go? In a way, this is less like one big question and more like an endless series of tiny questions that need to be answered in each moment. Learning to answer them in a way that leaves you feeling powerful and balanced is a magical skill that takes time and practice to develop.

In the meantime, checking with your gut feeling is a pretty decent way to mindfully navigate those tiny decisions. I also have another tool I sometimes use when I get stuck, which is a black and a white marble in a little bag. If I'm really on the fence about something, I use them for a simple kind of divination. Pulling out the black marble means severity (or I'll do the hard thing), while the white marble means mercy (erring on the side of indulgence). You could flip a coin in a similar way, with heads telling you to face the challenge versus tails for retreating. Sometimes, too, if you think you don't have a gut feeling about something, flipping a coin is also a good way to find out for sure. When you see what comes up, you may suddenly realize that you did know what you wanted after all.

ON DESIRE

Which brings us, in a roundabout way as we practice attention to awkwardly shaped emotions, back to desire. On some level, all of Witchcraft revolves around magic, and all of magic more or less revolves around desire—and yet, the magical process as I learned it at first can feel curiously bloodless in that regard. The traditional way of formulating intentions almost deliberately sidesteps desire with the instruction to speak as though the goal is already accomplished. For example, you might say, "I have a loving relationship," rather than, "I desire a loving relationship." This makes sense in terms of focusing on the goal rather than the current situation, and on a practical level I've gotten lots of great results with this method. It works! I absolutely continue to endorse this method, if it feels good and complete to you.

The more I practice and understand the value of staying present with uncomfortable sensations, though, the stranger I start to feel about shutting desire itself out of this process. I've started to think a lot about different ways of being with desire. On one hand, there's the way in which desire is experienced as a lack and a problem, as something to resist—and, for me, this thought and feeling of resistance does feel somewhat opposed to the kind of energetic flow that makes for good magic. On the other hand, though, there's a way of experiencing desire as a welcome and exciting, if somewhat poignant feeling. If this speaks to you, I suggest experimenting with ways to allow desire of that kind to become a kind of fuel for your magical process and intentions, too.

SPELLCASTING PART 4: RARE AND WONDERFUL INGREDIENTS

Traditional spells sometimes call for vanishingly rare ingredients, like unicorn blood or the dew collected at dawn from 10,000 flowers. At times these ingredients are a sort of code for more common components, designed to be crackable by those with the right experience—for example, a holly leaf was sometimes called a bat's wing because of the similar shape. There's something to be said, though, for the challenge and energetic investment of obtaining something rare and wonderful, whatever it might be. In a way, the effort and mystery that go into acquiring (or creating) that ingredient can become a crucial part of the spell.

When designing your own magical process, if you feel like it could use a little something extra, you might want to take this kind of ingredient as inspiration. Any component that's laboriously made by hand or obtained at great risk or price (financial or otherwise), during a certain phase of the moon or in a remote location can raise your stakes in the process significantly as well as weaving in additional symbolism and complementary energy. If you want to try something like this but aren't sure which direction to go, you could start by journeying to visit a spirit guide and asking what kind of rare ingredient would be appropriate for your goal.

Similarly, if you have the opportunity to gather any kind of materials during a particularly magical experience or in relation to a person, place, time or other quality you find particularly resonant or appealing, these materials are often worth keeping on hand for future projects.

ON LOVE SPELLS

Love spells deserve a special mention here as the final popular category of spell (and possibly the most popular category of all). By now, you can probably pretty much put one together for yourself. If you're not 100% sure you want to cast a spell on a particular person, casting a more general net to find love, for example by listing the qualities you desire in a partner or relationship, is a popular method and probably a good bet.

A lot of people suggest starting with work on self-love for greater confidence and general wellbeing. Because we tend to have such complex feelings about love and relationships, it might also be a good idea to do some groundwork on shadow topics—maybe some journaling on fears around love, or lingering resentment from past relationships. These can be productive places to start, but don't feel that you need to perfect anything before doing magical work to bring in a new relationship or any kind of love you want.

Of course, love spells can also be used to strengthen existing relationships, ideally with the participation of anyone involved.

MORE EXPERIMENTS WITH FIRE

1. Spend time with fire. Light candles and hang out around bonfires. Use saunas, sunbathe in moderation, and so on. How does it feel? How does it feel when you need more fire, and how can you tell when you've had enough?

1. Make art about it. What reminds you of fire? Wax, glue, metal, glass or other melting materials? Warm colors? Sparkling glitter? Another way to bring some fire to your art is to be more ambitious. What's a big, scary thing you just might consider making? Invite the energy of fire to help you get started.

2. Feeling blocked? Draw (or pretend to be) the wall, or whatever is blocking you. What does it feel like? What does it want? Maybe you can get it to leave you alone, or, if not, at least turn it into a new and different project.

3. Try things you've never tried before. Try things you've always wanted to try. Also try things that don't make sense, that you're not even sure whether you want to try or not. Refuse to be defined by what you expect yourself to want based on your past experience.

4. Do things that really challenge you physically. Something like a hard workout or a nature expedition that's at the edge of your tolerance can really shift your feelings of power and possibility, and eventually the reality of your capability as well.

5. Practice doing the hard thing first. If you make daily to-do lists, choose one thing (it can be a really small thing) that you're likely to put off indefinitely, and decide to do it before you do any of the other items. I've been pretty amazed at how quickly things can get done if I take one little step like this every day.

6. Consider traditional austerities like fasting, giving up a particular habit, or holding an all-night vigil. Like physical labor, these are efforts you can dedicate as an offering to a particular spirit or magical goal if you want.

7. Consider how openly you express your magical beliefs in the world. If you think your life or livelihood is really in danger then it's certainly reasonable to keep that kind of thing to yourself. If it's really quite safe, though, and you've kept those interests private because you're concerned about feeling awkward, ask yourself how well that's really serving you. Taking the step, if appropriate, to be more open about this aspect of your life can bring a feeling of increased integrity and power, as well as helping to pave the way for the magical people of the future.

The next page is a coloring page that you can use as part of a love spell. You can also download a printable version at http://lauragyre.com/creativerituals. Focus on your specific love-related intention while coloring the image, then use it however you like to complete your spell.

V. PUTTING IT TOGETHER

This is a pretty big and sprawling set of tools, and I hope you can use them to build something new and exciting. In case you're not sure where to go from here, though, I want to leave you with a few final notes about how I weave some of these things together into a relatively cohesive practice.

ON ELEMENTAL BALANCE

Now that you've read through and hopefully worked with each elemental process in some way, you probably have a better sense of which element(s) you feel strongest in. These strengths aren't bad, but in terms of developing greater balance (and, in my experience, generally increased power), it's a good idea to put more work into the areas that aren't as strong for you.

There are a couple of ways to approach this overall balance. The obvious one, I think, is to work the most on your weakest element, or maybe even the weakest two or three in proportion to how much they could stand to be strengthened. Alternately, If you're very strong in one element and much weaker in the other three, there's something to be said for focusing on your second strength or interest. This can be the quickest way to bring some degree of balance into your elemental field, and you can always work to fine tune it later.

There are also rare occasions when, if you need to change a lot and quickly, allowing yourself to get out of balance temporarily can actually be the best option. Once you've felt something shift, you can reconsolidate and start to move toward balance in your new situation.

For better or worse, elemental balance is a dynamic and infinitely refinable process, not a goal to be reached and then put on pause. Eventually, though, you should start to develop an intuitive feel for which direction you need to move at any given moment, and a greater sense of balance in motion.

TAROT FOR ELEMENTAL GUIDANCE

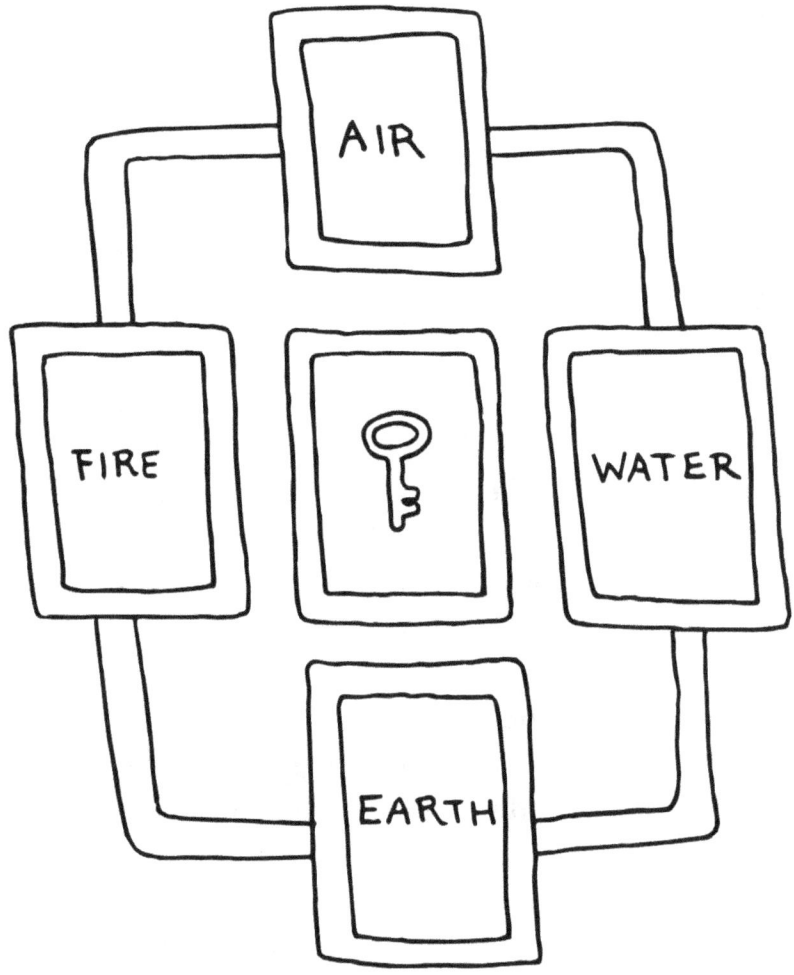

This is my favorite type of tarot spread. You can use it in relation to a specific question, or just to get an overview of your current situation. I often use it to determine what kind of practices I should focus on next.

Place one card in the direction of each element, and a fifth in the center. Each elemental card carries a message about your current relationship to that element. Generally, any reversed card indicates an element that could use some extra work. The center card is an additional key to finding balance in your current situation.

ON ELEMENTAL GUIDES

If you like trance, another good way to proceed is to do a series of journeys to meet a spirit guide for each one of the elements. Try to build ongoing relationships with these spirits, and visit whenever you could use some support in their areas or need some direction for further work.

Learning to trust your personal guides can be an important part of developing your own style of practice

ON CHECKING IN

This is a quick exercise I like to use in groups, to get people thinking about their elemental qualities. I also try to use it at least once a day, myself, for a kind of recentering:

First, take a couple of deep breaths to center yourself, then notice something that's on your mind right now (anything at all, it doesn't have to be particularly deep or meaningful). That's air. Then, tune in to your body and notice anything you can feel, hear, or otherwise physically sense at the moment. That's earth. Close your eyes, and see whether anything appears in your imagination. It could be an image, a sound or some other sensation, or even just a color that you see with your eyes closed—but in this case something that's just in your imagination, not in your physical environment. That's water. For fire, ask yourself what's missing for you right now. This could be something you desire, but it could also just be a sense of something you weren't consciously aware of until you took the time to look for it.

This check-in is something you can write about in your journal, or run through quickly in your mind (or out loud with a friend) any time you'd like to feel a little more magical or balanced.

ON BUILDING A PRACTICE

If you'd like to set a regular schedule to work on magical practice outside of casting spells when they occur to you, I suggest starting with the core practices described in each section: meditation for air, energy work and/or altar work for earth, trance and/or divination for water and moving toward challenges for fire.

Personally, I wrap all that up in journaling as a way to plan, create a bit of accountability and reflect on my experiences. My partner points out with some merit, though, that my focus on journaling may be largely an introvert thing. If you're more on the extroverted side, it might be really helpful to find a supportive friend who's willing to let you process by talking through your magical experiences, or better yet one who's willing to join you in those experiments.

If you have a bit more time I'd recommend a couple of other practices that narrowly missed the cut, too: having some sort of regular creative practice in your life, and playing around with ways to create sacred space. It's great to actively work on elemental balance, but a well-balanced set of basic practices also tends to lead toward increasing personal balance over time.

Opposite is a journal page that I designed to use as a daily check in with some elemental basics. You can use the rectangular space to draw a daily tarot card, an image from a dream or something similar. In the earth section, the body shape can be filled in with images representing your current physical sensations, and the circle can be used to record the weather or an observation from nature, plus the approximate phase of the moon. Feel free to make copies, download a printable version at http://www.lauragyre.com/creativerituals or use this as inspiration for your own type of record-keeping sheet.

A DAILY CHECK-IN PAGE

on my mind:

to do today:
1. _____
2. _____
3. _____

one thing I learned:

meditation? ☐

I dreamed:

divination or doodle →

happy thing

play time? ☐

outside:

I feel:

offerings? ☐
movement? ☐

power meter

I desire:

challenge / power source:

hard thing to do first:

done? ☐

BUILDING A SPELL

In each section we discussed techniques that can be used to cast spells, but now that all that framework is in place I wanted to briefly describe the overall process that I usually go through for spellwork. First of all, when I start to notice that I want to work with a desire I try not to rush it. Unless it's particularly urgent I hold on to a gentle awareness of that desire for a while, paying attention to when it shows up, how it really makes me feel and so on. Once I have a better sense of it I usually start journaling, writing about what I want, why I want it and any concerns I might have. Eventually I work toward clarifying an intention statement. At this point I sometimes do a tarot reading or a trance to consult a spirit guide, asking questions about what's blocking me from achieving my goal and what I need to focus on in order to create change.

After that, I'll start to design the actual spell or ritual. Sometimes that can involve a good bit of planning ahead, especially if it seems worth pursuing specific timing or any rare or pre-prepared components. I'll also watch during this time for any synchronicity or hints from the universe. Keeping an eye out for special magical materials or unusual opportunities often pays off!

I like to work in a calm, happy mood if possible, so I try to make sure I have plenty of time to do relaxing things like a ritual bath beforehand—though I wouldn't let that stop you from casting spells if it feels too impractical. Then I cast a circle (if it's that kind of day) or just sit down and get into a meditative mindset to do the work. Afterwards, I watch for signs.

I'm always, always curious to see what will happen next.

ON SPIRIT AND COMMUNITY

When I first started teaching this magical framework, I would talk about how you work on balancing the four elements and then spirit just sort of shows up. This is what I experience and it makes lots of sense to me on an intuitive level, but I once had a student in a class who wanted to know what this *spirit* was, exactly. I was kind of stumped so I asked him what he thought, and he said that it was connection. I'll admit that this is a growth edge for me. The more I work with this stuff, though, the more that I feel that he might have been onto something important.

It's not that spirit, in a general sense, appears or disappears from the world based on whether I'm doing my practice or not. It's my own ability to perceive my connection to something much, much bigger than myself that seems to wax and wane. This process of being connected is still incredibly mysterious, and certainly not one-sided. I'm learning things about it all the time, though. Like: an unusually graceful answer to the constant riddle of how hard to push ourselves might lie in community.

It occurred to me recently that both extremes of Mercy and Severity can feel weirdly individualistic on their own. On one hand, Severity says to push yourself and do your spiritual practice rigidly, no matter how your life is going or how you feel about it. Mercy, on the other, sometimes sounds a lot like it's saying that how you feel is the only thing that matters.

Connection might say that if there's a structure of relationship outside of yourself, for example a community, then spiritual practice doesn't just grind to a halt when you take a few days off from meditation. Of course, you can get at least part of the way to a similar place on your own. The more you build your life and your environment around magical practice, the more likely you are to come back to it again and again, and that can be a very individual thing. But, a community built around something is an extremely robust, highly interconnected and vital type of environment.

On a practical level, I've had some really great conversations around the material in this book, and pretty much all the exercises can be adapted to group work. Everything is a little different, of course, but the cool thing is that that can sort of work itself out. Just like magical practice can help an individual to develop more inner guidance, it can also help groups to evolve in interesting ways. This is something I'm just starting to work on, myself, but so far the results are compelling, and I'm extremely grateful to the folks who have joined me over the years in this exploration. If you start a group, I'd love to hear what you learn about this from your community.

TOWARD AN ETHICS OF WITCHCRAFT (PART 2)

Witchcraft is an overwhelmingly practical path, and a lot of what you'll learn along that path is experiential. Still, there are a few related beliefs I've somehow picked up along the way. I can't exactly say that these are Witchcraft teachings, but I also can't seem to shake the feeling that they're a part of the total package somehow.

Like: desire is mysterious and also holy. And, most avoidable harm seems to be caused by people making bad, out-of-alignment decisions about what to do with it, often due to reactive responses and a lack of useful information. Shaming yourself or others doesn't generally help with any of this. Punishment rarely does much good in the long term.

The good and bad news about this kind of belief is that when others cause problems for you, they have their own mysterious internal processes going on, too—and while you might not be able to rush them as much as you'd like, you *might* be able to speed up that natural process of growth (if and when you want to) by providing support—like some combination of resources, perspective, judgment-free attention and safe-ish space. In the meantime, of course, you're totally entitled to boundaries, to attempt to protect yourself and others from harm and to take a break (maybe even a permanent break) from trying to solve other people's problems.

If that last part sounds at all selfish to you, you should also know that I believe you have your own innately wonderful creative and transformative evolutionary process going on all the time, whether you're aware of it or not. Most of all, I've come to believe that the greatest gift you can give to yourself and the world is to value and nurture that totally unique, naturally unfolding, extremely magical process within yourself as it reaches out and touches every other part of the universe.

PERSONAL INSPIRATIONS I GENERALLY RECOMMEND INCLUDE:

Aidan Wachter's powerful, deceptively simple magical praxis

Peter Kingsley on ancient Greek philosophy and magic

On Becoming an Alchemist by Catherine MacCoun

The Sufis by Idries Shah

The Kabbalah of Light by Catherine Shainberg

Plant Intelligence and the Imaginal Realm by Stephen Harrod Buhner

Ensouling Language also by Stephen Harrod Buhner

Arnold and Amy Mindell's writing on Process Work

Rain Crowe's magical classes

Jan Fries on a variety of complex occult subjects

Shambhavi Saraswati on tantra

Belonging by Toko-Pa Turner

Brig Feltus on somatic practice and racial justice

Adrienne Maree Brown on magical approaches to organizing

The Tarot, Magic, Alchemy, Hermeticism & Neoplatonism by Robert Place

Tarot—the Open Reading by Yoav Ben-Dov

The Fyodor Pavlov Tarot

The Anima Mundi Tarot

Clementine Morrigan on trauma, sexuality, boundaries and magic

Melissa Tiers on hypnosis

Edward Butler on polytheism

Ramsey Dukes on chaos magic

www.ingramcontent.com/pod-product-compliance
Lightning Source LLC
Chambersburg PA
CBHW081616170426
43195CB00041B/2853